ROUTLEDGE LIBRARY EDITIONS:
HUMAN RESOURCE MANAGEMENT

Volume 22

# HIRING PRACTICES AND
# LABOR PRODUCTIVITY

# HIRING PRACTICES AND LABOR PRODUCTIVITY

MARIANNE J. KOCH

Routledge
Taylor & Francis Group

LONDON AND NEW YORK

First published in 1995 by Garland Publishing, Inc.

This edition first published in 2017
by Routledge
2 Park Square, Milton Park, Abingdon, Oxon OX14 4RN

and by Routledge
711 Third Avenue, New York, NY 10017

*Routledge is an imprint of the Taylor & Francis Group, an informa business*

*British Library Cataloguing in Publication Data*
A catalogue record for this book is available from the British Library

ISBN: 978-1-138-80870-6 (Set)
ISBN: 978-1-315-18006-9 (Set) (ebk)
ISBN: 978-1-138-28592-7 (Volume 22) (hbk)
ISBN: 978-1-315-26873-6 (Volume 22) (ebk)

**Publisher's Note**
The publisher has gone to great lengths to ensure the quality of this reprint but points out that some imperfections in the original copies may be apparent.

**Disclaimer**
The publisher has made every effort to trace copyright holders and would welcome correspondence from those they have been unable to trace.

# HIRING PRACTICES AND LABOR PRODUCTIVITY

MARIANNE J. KOCH

GARLAND PUBLISHING, INC.
NEW YORK & LONDON / 1995

Library of Congress Cataloging-in-Publication Data

Koch, Marianne J.
    Hiring practices and labor productivity / Marianne J. Koch.
      p.    cm. — (Garland studies on industrial productivity)
    Includes bibliographical references and index.
    ISBN 0-8153-2030-2 (alk. paper)
    1. Employee selection.   2. Employees—Recruiting.   3. Labor
productivity.    I. Title.   II. Series.
HF5549.5.S38K63   1995
658.3'112—dc20                                        95-18535
                                                          CIP

Printed on acid-free, 250-year-life paper
Manufactured in the United States of America

For Dan

# Contents

# Figures and Tables

# Preface

     Businesses in the United States spend thousands of dollars each year on each employee they hire, using a variety of recruitment and selection methods. Yet we don't know much about the effects various recruitment and selection practices have on the productivity of the workforce. That is, we do not know if some recruitment and selection techniques are better than others at producing productive, long-staying employees, while others do not. This book represents an effort to systematically study the characteristics that lead firms to choose the hiring practices they do, and the effects that various recruitment and selection methods have on labor productivity.

     This volume contains the updated research that originally constituted my doctoral dissertation at Columbia University. At the time that this research project was conceived and conducted (in the late 1980s), human resource management (HRM)—which encompasses the recruitment and selection functions studied in this volume—was growing in popularity as a field and was increasingly seen as a functional area within organizations which had the ability to significantly affect performance outcomes, including labor productivity. Jobs in the HRM field were increasing in both number and remuneration, and executives were endorsing the work of HRM professionals as that which could create a competitive advantage for their respective organizations. While claims about the effectiveness of HRM practices were being made in the popular press, there was, however, very little empirical evidence to back the claims that investments in hiring practices and other HRM functions would have a meaningful impact on productivity. Most evidence supporting the assertion that human resource management does matter was anecdotal in nature and involved a case study here and another one there. In short, there were no compelling studies or set of results from multiple sites to back up the popular notion that investments in human resource practices enhances firm performance. In this context, I undertook an empirical study to test whether or not human resource management practices—in this case, recruitment and selection practices—did, in fact, have a positive impact on the productivity of workers among a sample of U.S. businesses.

There were three purposes to this study. On the scholarly side, my purpose was to model, both theoretically and empirically, how certain human resource practices link to labor productivity, as well as to explain why some firms choose particular practices while others do not. To my knowledge, this had not been done previously. I limited my focus to hiring practices, as opposed to examining the whole of each organization's HR practices, in order to more clearly model the relationship between labor productivity and how the firm elects to manage its workers with respect to *one* decision (*i.e.,* hiring) as opposed to many. My purpose for conducting this research on the practical, or "real world," side was to test whether or not claims in the popular press concerning the link between HRM practices and firm performance were, in fact, sound. And finally, it was my purpose to move research in the HRM field from its traditional, "micro" orientation to focus on HR practices, their antecedents and effects on outcomes at the level of the organization.

This book contains the results of a research project in which the choice of recruitment and selection procedures and their relation to labor productivity for 495 U.S. businesses were investigated. The recruiting practices that were investigated included the types and number of recruiting sources used by each organization in the sample. Selection techniques that were studied included whether or not certain selection tests were used (ability tests, physical examinations, polygraphs, skill tests, and drug tests) to screen applicants, and how many interviews per hire were conducted. Finally, two administrative practices pertaining to the hiring function were considered: the formal planning for future hiring needs and the formal and regular evaluation of the recruiting and selection process.

Since this research was conducted, other empirical studies concerning this topic have begun to appear. Chapter One has been updated to include the research that has appeared since the time that this work took place. Researchers in the strategy field are focusing on HRM practices as the means to provide a sustainable competitive advantage to organizations. HRM researchers are modeling outcomes at the level of the organization, rather than at the individual level. And the results are indicating that, indeed, HRM practices do enhance productivity; organizations that make investments in HR practices enjoy a competitive advantage. This study represents one of the first efforts to show that HRM practices can improve firm performance, and the results have been replicated in other studies since then.

# Introduction

The recruitment and selection functions are important to study because (1) they are costly, (2) they determine the composition of a firm's workforce, and (3) recent demographic changes have tightened labor markets, thereby making it more difficult to hire a workforce that meets the firm's needs.

Workforce recruitment and selection are often expensive. According to the Association of Executive Search Consultants, United States firms spend $700 million annually on executive search alone. The Newspaper Advertising Bureau estimates that more than $2 billion is spent each year on newspaper recruitment advertising. It is estimated that recently, average costs per hire are $6,175 in the United States (Hartzell 1988). The high costs of recruitment and selection alone justify further research to improve our understanding of the relationship between these functions and outcomes of importance to organizations.

Recruitment and selection policies determine who will and will not be hired, and therefore, what the composition of the workforce will be. Since the workforce composition significantly affects firm performance, hiring policies and their differential effectiveness are important to understand.

Recent demographic changes in the United States labor force are raising average workforce age and increasing competition for workers. As the "baby bust" generation has been joining the workforce, the number of available young workers has diminished. At the same time, the workforce participation rates of women, immigrants, and older workers are increasing. The decline in the number of young workers, in conjunction with the increase in older workers, is causing an overall aging of the workforce. Such changes mean firms are now selecting workers from a pool with changing characteristics. Hiring methods that have worked well before may not continue to work as well. By the same token, declining birthrates, increasing restrictions on immigration, and the increasing incidence of two- career families, all make it more difficult for employers to hire the best possible workforce. This situation also calls for research which improves understanding of the recruitment and selection functions.

Unfortunately, although recruitment and selection are important areas for research, a review of the relevant literature reveals large gaps in our knowledge about how firms determine which practices to use and what effects variation in recruitment and selection strategies have upon an organization.

This book addresses two questions concerning the hiring process. (1) What factors determine the recruitment and selection practices used by firms in the United States today? and (2) Are there differential effects of recruitment and selection strategies on the productivity of a firm's workforce?

In the volume, I present a theoretical framework from which testable hypotheses addressing these questions may be derived. Subsequently, I develop and test empirical models of both the determinants of a firm's choice of recruitment and selection strategies, and the effects of these strategies on labor productivity. I utilize a data set put together at Columbia University to investigate these questions regarding two costly and crucial human resources management functions. It is hoped that this empirical analysis will fill some of the gaps that exist in our understanding of the hiring process.

The remainder of the book is organized as follows: in the first chapter, I give an overview of the hiring process, and review the literatures of several disciplines in which recruitment and selection have been studied. I also present a theoretical framework that can be used for the examination of these topics. Specific hypotheses to be tested are derived from the theory. In Chapter Two, I describe the data set to be used in the empirical analyses and demonstrate the rich variation in recruitment and selection methods currently being used in United States firms. The empirical model of the determinants of a firm's choice of recruitment and selection procedures is specified and tested in Chapter Three. The results of the empirical tests of the determinants model are also discussed. In Chapter Four, I test and discuss the effects of a firm's choice of recruitment and selection strategies on labor productivity. Finally, a summary and conclusions comprise Chapter Five.

# Acknowledgments

Many people helped to produce this book. Intellectually, I am indebted to my teachers at Columbia University. Professor Ann Bartel, my thesis advisor, helped me to develop the models and arguments in this book. She guided me through the many drafts of my doctoral thesis, always demanding rigor and thoroughness. She also worked patiently with me as I learned to use the computer to do statistical analyses. Professors David Lewin and John Delaney enriched my knowledge of the field of human resource management; this work benefited greatly from many hours of discussion with them. Other members of my dissertation committee included Professor Allen Barton of the Sociology department, and Dr. Mary Anne Devanna of the Columbia University Graduate School of Business; I am grateful for insights they offered that caused me to broaden my perspective concerning hiring practices. In addition, I was aided by Professor Casey Ichniowski in developing my ideas and especially, the empirical models.

This book would not have been possible without the support of Professors John Delaney, David Lewin, and Casey Ichniowski, who generously allowed me to use data they had collected. Further, I gratefully acknowledge Professor John Bishop for the use of his and Professors John Barron and Kevin Hollenbeck's model that appears as Figure 1.1 in this book. I thank Robert McKenzie, Lisa Pyeatt, and John McMackin for their editorial assistance in the production of this book, and my husband for his unflagging support throughout this project.

# Hiring Practices
# and Labor
# Productivity

# CHAPTER ONE

# Literature Review and Theoretical Framework

This chapter contains three sections. The first reviews the hiring process. The second discusses relevant portions of the human resource management (HRM) and labor economics literatures. The third presents a theoretical model for examining the antecedents and effects of a firm's choice of recruitment and selection strategies for hiring.

## SECTION A: OVERVIEW of the HIRING PROCESS

In the labor market, employers and individuals come together to make contracts to exchange compensation for labor services that the employer will use in the production of goods or services. The motivation for contracting for this exchange derives from the expected gains in which both parties will share.

The processes by which labor services are exchanged for wages are not costless, as they are assumed to be in classical economic theory (Oi 1962, Coase 1960, Williamson 1975). There are, for instance, transaction costs involved in the locating of individuals willing to sell their services (*i.e.*, recruitment), in the screening of applicants for hire prior to making employment decisions by employers (*i.e.*, selection), and in the search for job openings by individuals.

Transaction costs associated with forming the employment contract result from a need to gather information. That is to say, because of imperfect information, employers must locate individuals interested in taking available jobs. From this group, employers must identify which individuals have the knowledge, skills and abilities (KSAs) required for the job. Prospective employees must discover where vacancies are and determine which organizations have the characteristics they consider desirable.

Employers and individuals gather information through search processes. A representation of the basic processes (as described by Bishop, Barron and Hollenbeck, 1983) is included in Figure 1.1. Employers use various recruitment and selection procedures or strategies to locate potential employees and indicate to them the benefits of employment with the organization (1). Individuals search for job openings (2). Where there is interest on both sides, a selection decision is made (3). For those hired, the degree to which the match is successful (4) is revealed only after the employee has been evaluated on the job. If the individual is not selected, then he or she continues searching elsewhere (5).

Employers choose recruitment and selection strategies (6) based upon perceptions of how effective such strategies have been in the past (3 and 4 to 6). Likewise, the individual searches for work (2) using methods (7) that he or she perceives as likely to result in a successful match (3 and 4 to 7).

From Figure 1.1, it is evident that both individuals' and employers' search processes are integral parts of the hiring process. In order to understand the entire hiring process, we must investigate and understand its component parts.

## SECTION B: RESEARCH ON THE HIRING PROCESS

This section discusses what existing research tells us about the search processes of both employers and individuals, and points out gaps that remain. In both the labor economics and HRM literatures, emphasis has been placed on how individuals search for work (Devine and Kiefer 1993, Rynes 1991, Wanous and Colella 1989, Holzer 1987), but relatively little on the way *employers* choose their recruitment and selection strategies. This study attempts to fill that gap by exploring the determinants of employers' search strategies and their relationships to labor productivity.

FIGURE 1.1

The Search Process of Employers and Individuals[a]

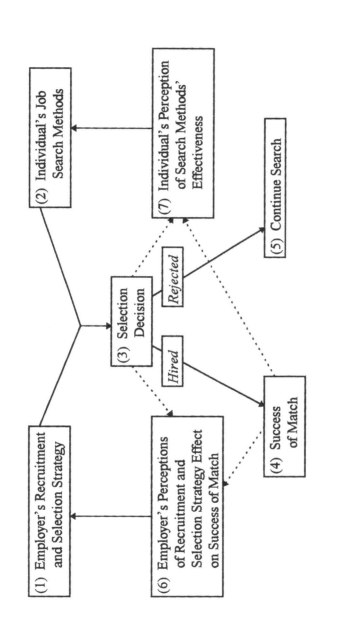

(1) Employer's Recruitment and Selection Strategy

(2) Individual's Job Search Methods

(3) Selection Decision

*Hired*

*Rejected*

(4) Success of Match

(5) Continue Search

(6) Employer's Perceptions of Recruitment and Selection Strategy Effect on Success of Match

(7) Individual's Perception of Search Methods' Effectiveness

[a] from Bishop, Barron and Hollenbeck (1983)

*Human Resource Management (HRM) Literature.* This section has two parts. The first concerns the HRM literature relating to recruiting sources. The second focuses on the HRM literature on employee selection, which has been produced predominately by Industrial/Organizational (I/O) psychologists.

     *Recruiting Sources.* Recruiting sources have typically been labeled as informal or formal (Rees and Schultz 1970, Reid 1972). The distinction has to do with how the recruiting is accomplished; informal recruiting sources are "those that do not involve the use of any outside organization or agency to arrange a contact between the employer and the job applicant" (Rees and Schultz 1970, p.199-200), or, of an "apparently hit-or-miss character" (Reid 1972, p.479). In studies, informal recruiting sources have included rehires, employee referrals, promotions-from-within (or, internal candidates), and direct applicants. Formal recruiting sources, in contrast, "make more use of established channels of job information" (*ibid.,*) and occur outside the organization. Examples of formal recruiting sources include newspaper advertising, college recruiting, private and public employment agencies, and search firms.

     The question—Which recruiting sources give individuals good information about potential matches?—has been explored. One hypothesis is that providing more realistic information to applicants about the job will result in better matches (Wanous 1977 and 1992, Quaglieri 1982). Realistic information "vaccinates" individuals against negative organizational characteristics and reduces expectations, and therefore, disappointment (Wanous 1992). Hence, realistic job previews are felt to result in higher employee satisfaction and longer voluntary tenure. Recruiting sources that have been hypothesized to offer realistic information include employee referrals, and current employees (*i.e.,* internal candidates) (Wanous 1992, Breaugh 1981, Caldwell and Spivey 1983).

     Many studies have tested the realistic information hypothesis (*e.g.,* Swaroff, Barclay and Bass 1985, Breaugh and Mann 1984, Taylor and Schmidt 1983, Caldwell and Spivey 1983). Most have found that informally recruited employees (*i.e.,* rehires, internal candidates, or employee referrals) remained longer, performed better, and were more satisfied than employees from formal recruiting sources (*i.e.*, college recruiting, newspaper advertisements, or employment agencies).

A second hypothesis about how recruiting source affects individual performance is called the individual differences hypothesis (Schwab 1982). Individual performance is thought to vary by recruiting source because different sources recruit applicants with distinctly different characteristics (Breaugh and Mann 1984, Taylor and Schmidt 1983).

*Employee Selection.* The I/O psychology literature concerning employee selection concentrates on measurement issues and the legal implications of using different selection instruments (Landy, Shankster and Kohler 1994).

Selection strategy research has been influenced by regulation of the hiring process. Courts have required that selection instruments and requirements be shown to be job-related when the employer is charged with discrimination (*Griggs Duke Power Company*, 401 U.S. 424, 1971). Researchers have been concerned with the way selection instruments predict performance both in training and on the job.

The validity of selection tests has been studied by Hunter and Schmidt in many articles (*e.g.*, Schmidt and Hunter 1983, Hunter and Schmidt 1983). They and their colleagues have used meta-analysis to demonstrate that validity study results are generalizable across jobs and organizations (*e.g.*, Schmidt, Hunter, Pearlman, and Shane 1979). Studies of the validity of selection devices other than tests have been conducted as well (*e.g.*, Dipboye 1992, Arvey and Campion 1982, Gatewood and Feild 1994, Milkovich and Boudreau 1988).

In addition to increased concerns about the validity of testing procedures, legal concerns also led human resource managers to question the economic benefits of various selection procedures. Researchers have responded with utility analysis. The "utility" of a selection procedure is the amount that a selection procedure improves the quality of individuals selected (Gatewood and Feild 1994). It was developed to provide a method for balancing the costs and benefits of implementing various selection procedures (Brogden 1949, Taylor and Russell 1934). Utility analysis is meant to show whether the improved validity of a new selection method is worth the additional cost (Scarpello and Ledvinka 1988). Utility is measured in terms of dollars. Critics of utility analysis argue that the component parts of the utility equation, in particular the standard deviation of performance (measured in dollars) and the validity of the selection instrument to be introduced, are so difficult to estimate that the results are often compromised (Scarpello and Ledvinka 1988, Cascio 1993).

In sum, the employee selection research concerns how well selection instruments predict the performance of prospective employees. It does not, however, deal with factors influencing a firm's decision to use particular selection methods. Because the research has focused on the individual as the unit of analysis and employed case studies, we know little about variation in choice of selection methods across firms. Similarly, utility analysis teaches us about possible productivity gains from selection innovations within one organization, but not across organizations.

*Planning and Evaluation of Recruitment and Selection Strategies.* The hiring process, from the employer's perspective, also includes certain administrative processes that concern both the planning and evaluation of the recruitment and selection functions. In the HRM literature, both human resources planning—the name given to the process of forecasting human resources needs for the organization—and the formal evaluation of the hiring process, are strategies hypothesized to improve the recruitment and selection processes, and thereby organizational performance. No formal theory has been developed to explain the way in which formal planning and evaluation affect performance, although a positive relationship is claimed to exist in the literature (*e.g.*, Walker 1992, Peters and Waterman 1980, Walker 1980). One study (Nkomo 1987), compared the economic performance (as measured by return on assets) of firms practicing human resources planning with those that did not. No significant differences in their comparative economic performance was found.

In summary, the HRM literature describes recruiting sources and selection instruments, and looks at the individual performance effects they have. The HRM research has not modeled the employer's choice of recruitment and selection methods however. This book contributes to research in HRM by modeling and testing the firm's choice of recruitment and selection strategies. In addition, it extends the performance effects research by investigating the effects of recruitment and selection strategies across firms, rather than within one firm, as previous HRM research has done.

*Labor Economics Literature.* Labor economists have studied the effects of imperfect information on both employer and employee job search (*e.g.*, Stigler 1962, Oi 1962, McCall 1970). In contrast to HRM researchers, labor economists, in their work on recruitment and selection strategies, have focused on market-level issues and outcomes. Most research has focused on employees' work search behavior (Holzer 1987, Bishop *et al.,* 1983). Optimal job search strategy studies have accounted for factors including choice of reservation wage (Salop 1973), risk aversion (Kohn and Shavell 1974), and intensity of search (Barron and Mellow 1979). Theoretical models of *employer* search behaviors have focused on market factors likely to affect the time needed to fill a job vacancy (*e.g.*, Albrecht and Axell 1984, Barron, Bishop and Dunkelberg 1985). Factors such as the supply of available labor and the availability of unemployment insurance have been shown to be associated with the time the employer will spend searching for a job candidate.

Unlike in the HRM field, labor economists have modeled employers' choice of recruitment and selection strategies. However, while labor economists have been interested in the factors that affect employers' investments in search, there has been less research on employer search strategies (Holzer 1987) than on individual search strategies. Limitations on data availability forced the focus on individual search. Data concerning employer search strategies were limited to relatively small geographic areas. For example, Malm (1954, 1955) and Rees and Schultz (1970) studied labor market conditions in the San Francisco Bay area and Chicago, respectively, and their relationship to the recruiting and selection strategies employed by firms of various sizes. They found that firms used more recruitment sources and searched across wider labor markets in times of tight labor supply.

Only recently have data been available which allow labor economists to investigate employers' search strategies across labor markets. For instance, more recent research (Holzer 1987, Barron, Black and Loewenstein 1987) has shown that larger firms spend more per hire on recruitment and selection than smaller firms. Likewise, work by Barron, Bishop and their colleagues (1983), and Holzer

(1987) are examples of recent work in which the determinants of employer search behavior are investigated.

Labor economists have also studied the effects of recruiting sources on the quality of the employment match between the individual and the firm. This line of research views the hiring process as an information problem: neither employer nor job applicant has enough information about one another to make good employment decisions. Consequently, employers will use signals of productivity, such as amount of education, to predict which applicants are more likely to succeed on the job (Spence 1973). Similarly, Rees (1966) made the distinction between formal and informal recruiting sources and hypothesized that informal recruiting sources would produce a better employment match; better information about the match would be received by both the employer and the job candidate. Empirical work by labor economists has supported the hypothesis that employee referrals, as a recruiting source, result in employees with higher productivity and longer average tenure than recruits from other sources (Reid 1972, Datcher 1983, Holzer 1987, Bishop, Barron and Hollenbeck 1983).

A shortcoming of the empirical work on the determinants and effects of hiring processes is poor quality of the available performance data. Outcome data have been limited to measures of supervisors' opinions of the performance of the most recently hired employee (Holzer 1987, Bishop, Barron and Hollenbeck 1983). More objective measures of performance at the firm level for *all* employees would improve our understanding of the effects of a firm's choice of recruitment and selection procedures.

*Needed Research.* This brief review of the HRM and labor economics literature concerning the hiring process indicates that we have paid much less attention to employer search strategies and how they are determined, than to worker job-search behaviors. We need to know more about employer hiring activities in order to more fully understand the hiring process, which involves the search behaviors of both employers and individuals.

With regard to hiring strategy research at the methodological level, there are several improvements that need to be made. First, researchers need better data to improve analyses and strengthen findings. Also, there is a need to study the antecedents and consequences of a firm's choice of recruitment and selection methods at the level of the firm; that is, we need to explore how and why firms use the recruitment and selection strategies that they do for all workers in the firm, not just the last one hired. To date, we know very little about differences in methods used to recruit and select different categories of workers.

In this book, I will explore the great variation that exists in firms' choices of recruitment and selection methods by investigating the following questions. (1) What are the determinants of a firm's choice of recruitment and selection strategies? (2) What are the effects of the firm's hiring strategies on the productivity of its workers?

## SECTION C: A THEORETICAL MODEL

As mentioned above, and to be illustrated in Chapter Two, there is great variation in the recruiting and selection procedures used by United States employers. These procedures vary widely by employee group in their costs to the employer. In this section, I will present a theoretical framework to explain both the variation in employers' recruitment and selection strategies and effects of these strategies on worker performance in the firm.

Let V equal the present value of the productivity of a new employee to the employer. From the employer's perspective, V is a random variable whose distribution is a function of the amount of information gathered about the new employee (Bishop, *et al.*, 1983). The employer gathers information by means of a chosen recruitment and selection strategy. The amount of information gathered varies across firms and for different types of jobs.[1]

The employer's objective in hiring is to maximize the expected value of the new employee's productivity, E(V), subject to the costs of employer search as given by his or her choice of recruitment and selection strategy.

When the employer wants to engage the labor services of workers, he or she decides how and where to recruit applicants, how many interviews to conduct and which selection tests, if any, to administer to the applicant pool.[2] These choices constitute the employer's recruitment and selection strategy. Using the adopted recruitment and selection strategy, the employer gathers a set of information for each applicant, represented by the vector $I_S$. This set of information can be summarized by what Bishop and colleagues (1983 p.8) called a "screening index of qualifications," which is denoted by $Q_S(I_S)$. The expected value of productivity of applicants with a screening index of qualifications greater than or equal to $q_S$ is given by $E(V|Q_S(I_S) \geq q_S)$. Individuals must have a screening index of qualifications score greater than $q_S^*$, (the reservation level of screening index of qualifications) in order to be considered for employment. $E(V|Q_S(I_S) \geq q_S)$ is increasing in $q_S$; that is, estimates of the expected value of the applicant's productivity are improved by the information gathered via the employer's chosen recruitment and selection procedures.

The information gathering process can be broken down into two types of search (Rees 1966)—*extensive* search and *intensive* search. Using the analogous situation of a buyer searching for the best price in the market for an item, Rees (1966) said, "A buyer can search at the extensive margin by getting a quotation from more than one seller. He can search at the intensive margin by getting additional information concerning an offer already received" (p.560). In the case of looking for new employees among candidates in the labor market, search at the *extensive* margin involves gathering information from more applicants before making a hiring decision—for instance, interviewing more candidates before hiring a new employee, or, using more recruiting channels to produce candidates. In contrast, search at the *intensive* margin involves gathering more information about each individual in the identified applicant pool prior to making job offers to some—for example, increasing the number of screening tests required of each job applicant, or preferring recruiting sources that reveal relatively more information about $E(V)$. Firms vary in their investments in extensive and intensive search strategies.

In a similar fashion, firms may invest in search through administrative activities that help to determine the precise manner in which extensive and intensive search will take place. Two such administrative activities are the formal *human resource planning* function by which the firm determines the amount and types of workers that will be needed to conduct business in the future, and the formal *evaluation of recruitment and selection strategies* employed by the firm.

Variation in characteristics of both the firm and its environment cause employers to invest differently in both extensive and intensive search strategies as well as administrative activities affecting the hiring process. The specific factors that determine the employer's investment in extensive and intensive search strategies, human resource planning and evaluation programs and their predicted effects on search strategies are the topics to which I now turn.

*The Determinants of Employer Search Strategies.* A firm's choice of recruitment and selection strategies used to gather information about the expected productivity of individuals in the applicant pool is a function of specific characteristics of the firm itself, its industry, and the labor markets from which it obtains job candidates.

*Firm-Specific Factors.* Firm-specific factors have to do with characteristics peculiar to the firm. A number of characteristics connected with the firm are likely to influence its choice of recruitment and selection strategy. The first of these firm-specific characteristics is the firm's size. Large firms are predicted to invest in recruitment and selection strategies more than small firms for a number of reasons. For one, large firms are usually more complex than small firms in job responsibilities and categories (Kossek 1987) which is likely to influence the firm's hiring policies and contribute to additional investment in search. Moreover, there are greater costs to larger firms in monitoring the performance of workers (Mellow 1982). That is, the difficulty associated with monitoring workers rises with firm size. This means that mistakes in hiring impose comparatively greater costs for large firms, which would in turn lead them to spend more in hiring so as to minimize mistakes (Bishop *et al.*, 1983). Mistakes in hiring are reduced by engaging in extensive and intensive search as well as by the careful planning and evaluation of recruitment and selection strategies. Further, larger firms can enjoy greater economies of scale in interviewing and other screening procedures than smaller firms, *ceteris paribus*, and therefore can be expected to search more both extensively and intensively for new employees.

For several reasons, the extent of unionization within a firm is another firm-specific characteristic likely to affect a firm's recruitment and selection policies. First, because unionized workers earn more on average than nonunionized workers (Freeman and Medoff 1984), the firm is expected to take greater care in hiring employees for union positions. That is, mistakes in hiring, are more costly to the firm for unionized than for nonunionized workers in the same job.

Because unionized employees have longer average tenure as well as receive higher average wages than nonunion employees (Freeman and Medoff 1984), employers incur both greater benefits and greater costs from unionized as opposed to nonunionized employees. Thus, a higher reservation level of screening index qualifications, $q_s^*$ will be required of workers in unionized positions. Therefore, it could be expected that employers will engage in more search, both at the extensive and the intensive margins, for unionized, relative to nonunionized, positions. Furthermore, it is reasonable to expect that increases in the extent of unionization of the firm's workforce leads the firm to invest more in both extensive and intensive search (Koch and Hundley 1994). There are, however, institutional characteristics of the hiring process for unionized positions that may mitigate the positive effect of unionism on the firm's investment in extensive and intensive search. In particular, collective bargaining agreements may specify that, *ceteris paribus*, the most senior internal candidates be given top consideration for jobs as they become available.[3] Or, employers may be obligated to hire from lists of job candidates who have taken written selection tests, in the order of performance on the test, for unionized positions. In 1977, eighteen percent of all collective bargaining agreements covering 1000 or more workers contained testing provisions pertaining to hiring, promotions and transfers (*Characteristics of Major Collective Bargaining Agreements* 1977 p.83). Hence, due to the presence of seniority clauses and testing provisions in collective bargaining agreements, other recruiting sources and selection strategies are less likely to be utilized for unionized positions. Therefore, although, all else being equal, it is expected that employers invest more in the search process for unionized workers relative to nonunionized workers, some employer search strategies, including the number and types of recruiting sources regularly used to generate applicants and the number of selection interviews conducted, are hypothesized to be negatively affected by the extent of unionism in the firm. Further, for the above stated reasons, it is also hypothesized that selection tests will be employed relatively more in highly unionized organizations.

Firms differ in their attitudes towards their employees. Each firm's attitude, or the extent to which the firm "values" its employees, is expected to have an effect on the firm's hiring policies. To "value" employees is an abstract concept that may be captured by certain policies or actions; for instance, firms that highly value their workers may grant them greater say in how business is to be conducted, or they may give workers great decision-making authority. To the extent that employees have greater responsibility in the firm, the firm's economic performance is directly affected by who those employees are. Recruitment and selection strategies, thus, take on relatively greater importance in firms where employees are highly valued by their employer. It is expected that the more the organization values its employees, as captured by the extent of employee involvement, the more it will invest in recruiting and selecting its workforce.

The provision of training to workers is also likely to influence a firm's recruitment and selection strategy. If one assumes that training increases an individual's productivity in proportion to the individual's initial ability, rather than increasing the productivity of all employees equally, then where there is more training offered to employees, the variance in expected value of labor will be greater (Bishop *et al.*, 1983). It pays for employers to have better information about who will be more productive (*i.e.*, who has a higher expected value of labor services) and will benefit proportionally more from the training offered. Consequently, it is expected that employers providing relatively more training to workers in the firm will search more both extensively and intensively for information about expected performance.

It must be noted that training availability may enhance recruitment and selection efforts by attracting more and more qualified applicants, and therefore could be considered endogenous to the firm's decisions regarding recruitment and selection strategy formulation. However, following Holzer (1987), it can be argued that the provision of training to employees is a longer run decision and one that is "embodied in contracts or bureaucratic practices that are not easily changed" (p.253). Thus, the availability of training can reasonably be taken to be exogenous to recruiting and selecting decisions in the short run.

The greater the firm's capital expenditures, the more physical capital there is, on average, for each employee to utilize in the production process. Thus, increased capital expenditures per employee predict greater average expected values of labor services. As a consequence, there are greater gains to extensive and intensive search for employers who invest heavily in capital equipment. Further, employers who have made investments in capital will require a workforce with the requisite skills to employ that capital in production and therefore they will need to locate specific types of skilled workers. This implies that an employer investing relatively more than other employers on capital expenditures will invest relatively more in recruitment and selection, in order to assure returns on his or her capital expenditures.

The last firm-specific characteristic to be discussed is the distribution of worker levels, and specifically, the amount of high-level workers in the firm. For higher level jobs in the organization, *ceteris paribus*, employers are expected to search relatively more both at the extensive and intensive margins, owing to the higher reservation level of screening index qualifications, $q_S^*$, attached to these jobs. Thus, the distribution of worker types in the organization is expected to have an effect on its investment in search strategies; in particular, it is expected that employers will engage in more search of certain types at the extensive margin, for high-level jobs relative to low-level jobs. In particular, investments in extensive search, as represented by interviews per hire, and number of recruiting sources used, are expected to rise with the percentage of high-level workers in the firm.

However, as Holzer (1987) points out, certain forms of search are not expected to be preferred by employers for the recruitment and selection of high-level employees. For instance, employers will use fewer selection tests on average to screen high-level employees for employment than low-level employees; as Glueck (1982) said, "(i)n general, tests are not frequently used in managerial selection" (p.313). Indeed, the fact that the most commonly used selection instrument for managers is the interview may be attributed to the fact that behavior for success in managers is complex and perhaps better tapped in interviews than tests (Campbell *et al.*, 1970). Thus, high-level employees are likely to be subjected to intensive search via avenues such as being interviewed by more people within the organization (*i.e.*, multiple interviews for each candidate) rather than being screened by means of selection tests.

Likewise, Rees and Schultz (1970) found that formal recruiting sources were used more for white-collar over blue-collar positions. Jobs requiring more skills and education may be more expediently filled by going to organizations that specialize in the recruitment of certain types of workers, such as search firms or private employment agencies (Holzer 1987). Moreover, employers studied by Rees and Schultz (1970) were found to believe that job candidates from certain recruiting sources—namely newspaper advertisements and private agencies—were of higher quality than candidates from other sources. For these reasons, it is expected that the relationship between the percentage of high-level workers in the firm and the use of selection tests and a preference for informal over formal recruiting sources will be negative, while being positive for interviews per hire and the number of recruiting sources used, as well as for the administrative activities of human resource planning and evaluation of recruitment and selection policies.

*Industry Characteristics.* The hiring process and firms' investments in recruitment and selection differ from one industry to the next. There are several reasons why this is so. First, pay structures differ by industry; starting salaries and pay increases are not uniform across firms in different industries for reasons including compensating differentials. Second, hiring standards vary across industries (Malm 1955, Reynolds 1951); educational and skill requirements for positions of a given level in different industries may demonstrate great variation. And third, traditional approaches to recruitment and selection are likely to show variance from one industry to the next; whereas hiring "at the gate" is common for hiring low-level workers in manufacturing (Malm 1954), firms in the financial services area may recruit largely from newspaper advertisements for low-level positions. All of these differences derive, in part, from differing firm needs with respect to worker skills, and, in part, from history—that is, simply the way the hiring process evolved over time and developed nuances peculiar to the industry.

Because wage structures and hiring standards vary by industry, it is expected that the extent which firms in one industry seek information about job candidates at both the extensive and intensive margins, will significantly differ from firms in other industries. Likewise, because higher wages and/or lower required qualifications both may serve as substitutes for search, industry differences must be controlled for in order to measure the effects of other factors on the firm's choice of certain recruitment and selection strategies.

       *Labor Market Factors*. The third category of factors likely to influence a firm's choice of recruitment and selection methods pertains to the characteristics of the labor markets from which the firm hires.

       To begin with, there are laws which directly influence the ways in which employers recruit and select workers. Among these laws, Title VII of the 1964 Civil Rights Act arguably has the greatest impact. There, it states that employers are proscribed from discriminating in both hiring and promotion decisions against individuals on the basis of race, religion, color, sex or national origin. Because of this, employers must insure that their recruitment and selection methods do not infringe on the rights of members of these protected classes. This implies that the composition of the labor market, in terms of the characteristics which are protected by law (*i.e.*, race, sex, etc.), from which the firm does its hiring will have an impact on the firm's recruitment and selection strategies. Specifically, it is expected that as qualified candidates from protected classes decline as a percentage of the available labor market, the firm will invest more in search in order to insure that it meets equal employment opportunity requirements. Firms hiring from labor markets with a high percentage of both white and male workers will have a relatively more difficult time hiring qualified minorities and women than firms searching for workers in more racially and sexually balanced labor markets. As a result, it is expected that firms operating in labor markets with a high percentage male and/or white workers will be more likely to engage in formal planning and evaluation of staffing policies, as well as more extensive and intensive search.

       The average education level of workers in the pool from which the firm hires is also expected to affect the firm's investment in search. A highly educated labor force is able to command higher compensation, *ceteris paribus*, because of investments it has made in human capital (Becker 1975). Likewise, firms gain in increases in expected productivity from a more educated workforce, other things equal. Therefore, as the educational credentials of the applicant pool increase, firms have a greater incentive to avoid making hiring mistakes, since they have relatively more to lose when employment mismatches occur. This, in turn, leads firms to search more for information about expected productivity at both the extensive and intensive margins, as the education level among the available job candidates rises.

A number of specific hypotheses have been posed in this section regarding factors likely to influence an employer's choice of search strategies. To summarize them, it is expected that a firm's investment in extensive and intensive search will increase with firm size, the extent to which the firm values its employees, and its capital expenditures. The extent of unionization of workers is expected to negatively affect the number and types of recruiting sources used in hiring, as well as the number of employment interviews conducted per hire. Unionization of the organization is further hypothesized to be positively related to the number of selection tests used. The percentage of high-level workers in the organization is hypothesized to positively predict both extensive and intensive search strategies with the exception of the usage of selection tests and a preference for informal in lieu of formal recruiting sources, upon which they are expected to have a negative influence. It is likewise predicted that the firm's investment in both extensive and intensive search, as well as its formal planning and evaluation of hiring policies, will increase with the percentages both white and male of workers in the labor market, and with the average level of education among potential employees. These hypotheses will be tested and the results discussed in Chapter Two.

*The Effects of Employer Search Strategies on Labor Productivity.* This theoretical framework also addresses the effects of a firm's choice of recruitment and selection strategies on the performance, or productivity, of employees. In this section, I will discuss the relationship between, and outline the expected effects of recruitment and selection strategies on labor productivity in the firm.

Recall that estimates of the expected value of the applicant's productivity are improved by the information gathered via the employer's chosen recruitment and selection procedures. As stated above, these procedures can be broken into extensive and intensive search methods.

*Extensive Search.* Search at the *extensive* margin means gathering more information about the relevant labor market and the potential candidates contained therein. That is, the number of applicants screened per hire represents employer extensive search. Raising the reservation level of screening index of qualifications, $q_S^*$, increases the expected number of applicants screened prior to making a hire, or the extent of extensive search. This increase in the expected number of applicants to be screened per hire is hypothesized to increase the expected value of the new hire's labor productivity, $E(V)$.

Extensive search can also be measured by the number of recruiting sources the employer regularly uses to generate applicants for job vacancies. Because an employer cannot control the number of applicants produced by recruiting sources in which the candidate or referral makes initial contact (*e.g.*, walk-ins, or employee referrals), he or she must often use multiple recruiting sources simultaneously to ensure an applicant pool of adequate size. This is especially the case where job vacancies in the organization can alter or even halt production, and where having someone to do the job at all times is crucial. In this sense, the number of sources regularly used by the organization for the generation of employment candidates also measures extensive search. As the firm uses more recruiting sources on a regular basis, the average expected value of productivity is expected to increase.

*Intensive Search.* In contrast, search at the *intensive* margin refers to the amount of information gathered about each of the applicants in the pool before making a hiring decision. Intensive search can be measured in a variety of ways; one way is by the number of screening devices or selection tests administered to each applicant prior to extending an offer of employment to any candidate. The expected value of a new employee's productivity increases with the set of information gathered for each applicant, $I_S$, because of the increased accuracy of the prediction.

Beyond the number of selection instruments administered to each applicant, the intensity of employer search may also be measured by the use of certain recruiting sources that provide better information about applicants. That is, to the extent that some recruiting sources are more accurate than others in predicting an individual's expected productivity, the employer will maximize productivity by preferring these recruiting sources.

There are two ways in which recruiting source could systematically be related to expected value of labor services. First, recruiting sources that give the employer information concerning the applicant's ability to succeed on the job that competing employers cannot observe or know, will improve labor productivity and firm profits (Bishop *et al.*, 1983). Employee referrals are an example of a recruiting source that offers the firm information about the individual that other firms are not likely to know nor able to discern (Rees 1960, Quaglieri 1982, Reid 1972). The employee making the referral offers the employer information about how the individual matches the organization and any special knowledge, skills and abilities (KSAs) that he or she may bring to the job (Wanous 1992, Reynolds 1951). Such information is not likely to be tapped by the selection devices used by other employers.

A recruiting source may also be better at predicting expected value if it is related to some characteristic that gives the applicant a comparative advantage in that firm (Bishop *et al.*, 1983). Examples of this type of characteristic include: knowledge or skills that the hiring firm-specifically needs, the ability to work particularly well with the firm's current workforce, or increased likelihood of remaining with the firm (possibly because of having worked there already or having friends or family in the organization). Employee referrals or in-house applicants are likely to have characteristics such as those mentioned above. For these reasons, it is expected that using employee referrals or in-house candidates will give employers an advantage in hiring that will allow them to improve the average expected value of their workforce.

*Administrative Policies concerning Recruitment and Selection Strategies.* Two administrative policies that are a part of employers' hiring processes, but not investments in extensive and intensive search strategies *per se*, are formal human resource planning (HR planning) for staffing and the formal evaluation of the recruitment and selection policies of the firm. The planning for and evaluation of the hiring process represent investments in employer search that will affect employee performance in the following ways.

HR planning involves designing policies and programs which specifically focus on the number and type of people to be employed by the organization (Scarpello and Ledvinka 1988). HR planning is hypothesized to be positively associated with firm performance (Walker 1992). Through HR planning, the firm more clearly identifies the specific types of workers that are needed and projects exact manpower needs, given organizational objectives. By planning for and hiring the right types and amounts of employees to meet organizational goals, the quality of the employment match is enhanced and labor productivity rises.

Formal evaluation of hiring policy allows for learning, or, the incorporation of hiring policies and programs that have been demonstrated to be beneficial to hiring outcomes. Formal and regular evaluation of recruitment and selection strategies also allows for the discontinuation of strategies that have not produced good employment matches for the organization in the past. This important feedback loop is expected to enhance employers' investments in extensive and intensive search and improve the quality of employee performance.

In sum, I can make the following predictions about how employers' investments in extensive and intensive search will affect the performance of the workforce from the theoretical framework presented here. First, the expected value of labor productivity will increase with extensive search as measured both by the number of interviews conducted per hire and the number of recruiting sources the employer uses. Second, the expected value of labor productivity will increase with intensive search as measured by the number of selection instruments administered to each candidate and by using informal recruiting sources to generate candidates. And third, administrative policies that concern the hiring process—specifically, the formal planning of the recruitment and selection functions, and the formal evaluation of these functions, as well—will have a positive effect of the performance of workers in the firm.

*Hypotheses to be Tested.* From this theoretical model, a number of testable hypotheses are generated. I will summarize here the specific hypotheses to be tested.

Concerning the determinants of the firm's recruitment and selection strategies: (1) Extensive search, as measured by (a) the number of interviews per hire and (b) the number of recruiting sources used, is expected to be positively influenced by firm size, the percentage of high-level workers in the firm, the extent to which the firm values its employees, the percentages of whites and males and the education level of individuals in the labor force from which the firm hires, and the amount of its capital expenditures, and negatively influenced by the extent of unionization of the firm. (2) Intensive search, as captured by (c) the number of selection tests administered and (d) a preference for informal over formal recruiting sources, is expected to be positively influenced by firm size, the extent of unionization of the firm (for (c) only), the extent to which the firm values its employees, the percentages of whites and males and the education level of individuals in the labor force from which it hires, and the amount of its capital expenditures, and negatively by the percentage of high-level workers in the firm and the extent of unionization of the firm (for (d) only). (3) It is hypothesized that firms will increase their formal planning and evaluation of hiring policies with increases in firm size, the extent of unionization of the firm, the extent to which they value their employees, the percentages of whites and males and the education level of individuals in the labor force from which they hire, the percentage of high-level workers in the firm, and the amount of their capital expenditures. These hypotheses will be tested and the empirical findings discussed in Chapter Two.

The specific hypotheses generated regarding the effects of recruitment and selection strategies on labor productivity are: (1) the number of interviews conducted per hire, and the number of regularly used recruiting sources will both improve labor productivity; (2) the number of selection tests administered to candidates, and the preferences for informal over formal recruiting sources will have a positive effect on labor productivity; and (3) formal HR planning for staffing and selection, and the formal evaluation of recruitment and selection strategies will each have a positive effect on the productivity of labor. An empirical model to formally test these hypotheses is developed in Chapter Three, where the results are also reported and discussed.

The next chapter makes use of a unique data set to show the substantial variation in the recruitment and selection strategies of employers in the United States today. This data set will also be used to test the hypotheses outlined above.

## NOTES

1. It is assumed that wages and hiring standards are fixed during the recruitment and selection process. This assumption is necessary because higher wage offers and/or lower hiring standards can be used as substitutes for increased search (Stigler 1962); this assumption also prevents the employer from making a unique wage offer to each applicant based upon his or her estimation of each applicant's expected productivity. Because of the presence of internal labor markets within organizations which are characterized by rules and customs concerning pay scales and requirements for jobs (Doeringer and Piore 1971), the assumption of fixed wages and hiring standards during the hiring process is not unreasonable. In fact, most organizations have fixed ideas of what each job's requirements and qualifications are, and customary starting wages for each job (Osterman 1984). In addition, this analysis excludes employment contracts for jobs in which wages are not set until after the individual's level of productivity has been revealed by time on the job. Thus, there is a gain to information regarding the applicant's productivity level that is collected by the employer *prior* to hiring. Because for the vast majority of jobs, wages are specified before a new employee begins to work, this assumption does not exclude many jobs.

2. It is further assumed that employers are able to produce applicants from their chosen recruiting sources (i.e., that there is no labor supply shortage).

3. A 1970 BLS bulletin reported that seniority is a factor in promotion in 90 percent of manufacturing and 43 percent of non-manufacturing agreements (Kochan 1980, p.365).

# CHAPTER TWO

# Description of the Data

There are two aims to the current chapter. First, by means of a unique data set, I will demonstrate that there is great variation in the recruitment and selection strategies across firms. And second, more specifically, I will compare the levels and types of employer investment in extensive and intensive search for high-level versus low-level jobs, and for union versus nonunion positions.

The next section describes the sources of the data used in the analysis. The following section describes the extent and type of variation in U.S. firms' recruitment and selection strategies.

## SECTION A: THE DATA SET

To investigate the variation in a firm's choice of recruitment and selection methods, this study makes use of a unique data set concerning human resource practices in United States corporations. It, and other sources used to collect information for control variables, are described below.

*Recruitment and Selection Practices Data.* The data set utilized in this study comes from a survey of United States firms and gathered extensive information about the human resources management practices in these firms. The survey information specifically concerning each firm's recruitment and selection practices makes up the subset of data employed in these analyses. The twenty-four page survey that generated the data set was administered by members of the Industrial Relations Research Center at the Columbia

Graduate School of Business during 1986 and 1987.[1] The survey instrument was sent to top human-resource officers of the firms that were contained in the 1985 Compustat II Industry Segment files. A total of 495 usable responses was obtained.[2] It should be noted that the unit of analysis in the Compustat II Industry Segment files is the *business unit*, not the firm as a whole. Because a large number of United States firms are highly diversified today, using the business line or unit, as opposed to the entire firm, as the unit of analysis permits more accurate classification of the unit by industry.

Because some questions were left blank on the survey by those filling it out, the data set is not complete. Blanks in the returned surveys were entered as missing data. The data from the survey concerning the employers' recruitment and selection practices are used in this study to create both the dependent variables in the determinants model and some of the explanatory variables in the performance model. Other data from the Columbia HR survey are employed as control variable measures in both models. These variables will be described below in Chapters Three and Four.

*Performance Data.* Measures of labor-force performance used to construct the dependent variables in the performance-effects model of this study (see Chapter Four) were compiled from Standard and Poor's Compustat II Industry Segment computer database. These Compustat II data are collected for each business unit within each firm in the sample. The gathered data are originally published in each firm's annual report and/or its 10-K report as required by the Securities and Exchange Commission. Compustat II data from the years 1986 and 1983 are used in the book to develop economic performance measures as well as some independent variables and control measures for both models. There are few missing observations. However, it should be noted that the Compustat II identification codes for individual business lines change, in some cases, from one year to the next, making the compilation of longitudinal economic data for all observations in the sample difficult.[3]

*Control Variables Data.* The remaining independent variables used as controls in both the determinants and the performance models were obtained from several sources. One source of information used to create control variables was the Columbia Human-Resources survey described above. In this survey, beyond data concerning its human resource policies, each business unit provided information about organizational characteristics such as number of employees, and the extent of unionization. This information was used to create some independent variables used as controls in the analyses.

Information descriptive of the labor market characteristics for each business unit's industry was gathered from the Current Population Survey for 1985. The precise variables created from these data sources will be described in detail in Chapters Three and Four.

It is by the use of these data and the models developed in Chapters Three and Four that the antecedents and performance effects of hiring practices currently employed by United States firms will be empirically investigated for this study. I turn now to a description of the recruitment and selection strategies employed by business units in the sample.

## SECTION B: VARIATION in RECRUITMENT and SELECTION PRACTICES in FIRMS in the UNITED STATES

*Firms in the Sample.* Some descriptive statistics of the firms[4] in the sample are given in Table 2.1. Let us start with the industrial distribution; the sample contains observations in each of six major industrial groups in the Standard Industrial Classification (SIC) system. Most firms in the sample belong to the manufacturing sector (46.1 percent). The next largest representation is the transportation (including communications) industry, with approximately seventeen percent. Firms in the finance, insurance, and real estate industries comprise twelve percent of the sample, as do firms in the services industry. The remainder of the sample is made up of firms in the agriculture, mining, construction and trade industries.

The average organization in the sample has 6,082 employees, although twenty-nine percent of firms have between one and five hundred employees. Almost one half (45 percent) of the business units have more than one thousand employees, and nearly twenty percent have five thousand or more. The range of size in the sample is between 2 and 238,000 employees. The sample, thus, preponderantly represents large firms (*i.e.*, those with more than 500 employees).

TABLE 2.1

*Descriptive Statistics of Firms in the Sample (Standard Deviation=SD)*

| Variable | Percent | N | Mean % | SD |
|---|---|---|---|---|
| **Industry Group** | | | | |
| Agriculture, Mining, Construction | 6.5 | 32 | | |
| Finance, Insurance, Real Estate | 11.9 | 59 | | |
| Manufacturing | 46.1 | 228 | | |
| Transportation | 16.6 | 82 | | |
| Trade - Wholesale and Retail | 7.5 | 37 | | |
| Services | 11.5 | 57 | | |
| **Size (Number of Employees)** | | | 6082.1[a] | 18853.2 |
| 2 - 99 | 12.6 | 53 | | |
| 100 - 499 | 29.4 | 124 | | |
| 500 - 999 | 13.3 | 56 | | |
| 1000 - 4999 | 25.2 | 106 | | |
| 5000 - 9999 | 5.7 | 24 | | |
| 10000 - 49999 | 11.6 | 49 | | |
| 50000+ | 2.4 | 10 | | |
| **Unionization** | | | | |
| Nonunion Firms | 40.3 | 170 | | |
| Percent of employees unionized | | | 18.1 | 26.6 |
| Percent of employees nonunionized | | | 81.9 | 26.6 |
| **Firms With Workers in Categories** | | | | |
| Managers | 100.0 | 415 | 15.1 | 10.2 |
| Unionized Professional/Technical | 10.3 | 50 | 1.2 | 5.6 |
| Nonunion Professional/Technical | 95.6 | 394 | 23.3 | 19.8 |
| Unionized Clerical | 16.0 | 77 | 2.4 | 8.6 |
| Nonunion Clerical | 97.8 | 407 | 20.1 | 18.4 |
| Unionized Production/Manufacturing | 34.1 | 157 | 14.7 | 23.0 |
| Nonunion Production/Manufacturing | 68.4 | 294 | 25.2 | 27.0 |
| | | | | |
| Percent High-level workers[b] | | | 38.9 | 22.2 |
| Percent Low-level workers[b] | | | 61.2 | 22.2 |

[a] Mean number of employees, not mean percentage.
[b] High-level workers includes managers, professional and technical workers; Low-level workers includes clerical, manufacturing and production workers. N=495.

Forty percent of the business units in this sample have no unionized workers (n = 170). Eighteen percent of the workers in the average business unit are covered by collective bargaining. Approximately ten percent of the firms have unionized professional or technical employees, sixteen percent have unionized clericals, and over thirty-four percent of the firms employ unionized manufacturing or production workers. On average, only one percent of all business lines' workers are unionized professionals or technical workers; 2.4 percent are unionized clericals, and almost fifteen percent are unionized manufacturing and production workers.

Managers account for fifteen percent of the employees in the average organization in the sample. Every organization in the sample reported having managerial employees. Almost all of the firms also reported employing nonunion clericals (97.8 percent) and nonunion professional or technical workers (95.6 percent).

Employees are categorized in either high-level or low-level jobs. The high-level category includes managers, professional and technical workers. The low-level category includes clerical, manufacturing, and production workers. When employees are categorized as high or low-level employees, it is found that the average firm has close to forty percent high-level employees and 61.2 percent low-level employees.

Thus, the overall picture of the average business unit in this sample is of one that is large, in the manufacturing industry, not largely unionized, and with a majority of low-level workers.

*Use of Recruitment and Selection Procedures by Firms in the Sample for Various Worker Categories.* Let us now look at the distribution in the use of various recruitment and selection practices by the business lines in the sample. Table 2.2 provides a summary of the usage of different employer search strategies for seven employee categories: managers, unionized professionals and technical workers, nonunionized professionals and technical workers, unionized clericals, nonunionized clericals, unionized manufacturing and production workers, and nonunionized manufacturing and production workers.

Table 2.2 also presents information on the percentages of firms that practice human resource planning for staffing, and that engage in the formal evaluation of the staffing function. These last two items tell us about firm-wide administrative policies which affecet the recruitment and selection of all workers in the organization, and are therefore not measured separately for each of the seven groups described above. Looking at the numbers for these two administrative practices, we see that 86 percent of the firms in the sample formally evaluate their recruitment and selection functions, but that only 42 percent of them have a policy of formal human resource planning for recruitment and selection. These numbers suggest an overall preference among the firms in this study for a reactive, as opposed to a proactive, approach to administering the hiring function. That is, the business units in the sample adjust their hiring procedures or strategies *post hoc*, as opposed to formally planning prior to hiring.

TABLE 2.2

*Mean Usage of Recruitment and Selection Strategies by Firms in the Sample for Various Worker Categories*

| Variable | Managers | Professional or Technical Workers | | Clerical Workers | | Production or Mftg Workers | |
|---|---|---|---|---|---|---|---|
| | | U | NU | U | NU | U | NU |
| Extensive Search | | | | | | | |
| Mean Interviews per Hire | 7.35 | 7.68 | 6.45 | 4.82 | 5.47 | 4.41 | 4.84 |
| Number of Recruiting Sources Used | 4.76 | 4.34 | 5.55 | 3.82 | 4.52 | 3.63 | 4.28 |
| Intensive Search | | | | | | | |
| Number of Selection Tests Given | 0.94 | 1.93 | 0.99 | 2.26 | 1.48 | 1.81 | 1.19 |
| Percent of Informal Recruiting Sources Used | 0.39 | 0.43 | 0.34 | 0.49 | 0.43 | 0.49 | 0.45 |

Administrative Practices
  Percent of Firms that do HR planning for Staffing   41.9%

  Percent of Firms that Formally Evaluate Staffing   85.7%

NOTE: U = Union; NU = Nonunion. Sample size ranges from 308 to 489 for nonunion workers, and from 44 to 166 for unionized workers due to missing data.

In the Columbia HR survey, firms were asked whether or not they regularly used nine different recruiting sources to identify and recruit employees. Recruiting sources are the names given to the places or methods by which an employer and applicant locate one another. Recruiting sources inquired about in the Columbia HR survey include: newspaper advertisements, recruiting at undergraduate schools, recruiting at graduate or professional schools, search firms, government employment agencies, private employment agencies, using employee referrals, walk-ins (also known as direct applicants), and using promotions-from-within. Recall that recruiting sources are divided into two groups: formal and informal. Informal recruiting sources include employee referrals and promotions-from-within; the others can be categorized as formal recruiting sources. Table 2.2 shows both the number of recruiting sources regularly used to locate workers of different types and job levels, and the extent to which informal recruiting sources are preferred to formal recruiting sources for the various employees groups. On average, the most recruiting sources—about six—are used to find nonunionized professional or technical workers. The fewest recruiting sources are used to find unionized production workers and unionized clericals (roughly four each). It appears that informal recruiting sources are preferred to more formal ones most for unionized clericals and production workers. Further, preference for formal recruiting sources is highest for nonunionized professional and technical workers and managers.

The selection tests whose usage was investigated in the Columbia HR survey include: formal skill tests, aptitude tests, polygraphs,[5] drug tests, and physical examinations. The number of selection tests regularly administered to job applicants is one of the measures of intensive search to be investigated in this study.

The raw usage data indicate that unionized clerical workers are given more than two of the five possible selection tests on average—the greatest number of selection tests administered among all the worker groups. With just less than two regularly administered selection tests each, unionized professional and technical employees and production workers rank next. The fewest tests are used in the selection of nonunionized professional and technical employees, and managers.

The patterns evinced by this table demand a closer look at the variation in recruitment and selection practices for two groups of workers—high versus low-level workers, and unionized versus nonunionized workers. High-level workers include managers and professional and technical employees. The low-level group includes clericals and production or manufacturing workers. The unionized versus nonunionized groups include all employee groups, with the exception of managers—that is, the professional or technical, clerical, and manufacturing or production workers.

From Table 2.2, it appears that there are distinct differences in the amount of extensive and intensive employer search invested in the hiring of high versus low-level employees. The data were thus aggregated to test this hypothesis. Recall that it was predicted in the last chapter that employers would expend more effort on search for high-level workers over low-level workers, *ceteris paribus*.[6]

In Table 2.3, we can observe the differences in usage of recruitment and selection strategies for high and low-level worker categories. The raw data indicate both greater extensive and intensive search for high-level jobs relative to low-level jobs. Specifically, firms conduct more interviews per hire for high-level jobs than for low-level jobs (approximately 7 compared to 5 respectively, on average).

TABLE 2.3

*Mean Usage of Recruitment and Selection Strategies by Business Units in the Sample for High-level and Low-level Job Categories*

|  | High-level Jobs[a] | | Low-level Jobs[a] | |
|---|---|---|---|---|
|  | Mean Usage | N | Mean Usage | N |
| Extensive Search | | | | |
| Mean Interviews per Hire | 6.94 | 470 | 5.07 | 461 |
| Number of Recruiting Sources Used | 5.10 | 490 | 4.25 | 488 |
| IntensiveSearch | | | | |
| Number of Selection Tests Given | 1.02 | 488 | 1.50 | 487 |
| Percent of Informal Recruiting Sources Used | 0.37 | 488 | 0.35 | 484 |

[a] High-level job category includes managers, professional and technical workers; Low-level job category includes clerical, manufacturing and production workers.

Likewise, business units in the sample use more, but not significantly more, recruiting sources regularly to recruit high-level workers than to recruit low-level employees.[7] Approximately five recruiting sources are regularly used to locate applicants for high-level jobs, as compared with four recruiting sources regularly used for low-level job openings.[8] As was noted above, certain of these recruiting sources, especially search firms, tend to specialize in the recruitment of high-level employees.[9]

      Although the raw data indicate that employers will invest relatively more in intensive search for the recruitment and selection of high-level workers, differences for high versus low-level workers were not statistically significant. Specifically, intensive search, as captured by a preference for informal recruiting sources was found to be greater, but not significantly greater, for high-level versus low-level employees; whereas, the number of pre-employment selection tests used for screening high-level employees is lower, but, again, not significantly lower, than the number used in the selection of low-level workers. As predicted, the data show that employers use fewer selection tests on average to screen high-level employees for employment than low-level employees; when the selection tests are disaggregated, skill and aptitude tests are both used significantly more for the selection of low (66.2 and 27.5 percents, respectively) than high-level employees (24.7 and 21.8 percents, respectively).[10]

      Table 2.4 reports the differences in usage of recruitment and selection strategies for union versus nonunion workers. From the mean usages reported in Table 2.4, it appears that employers do, in fact, invest less in extensive search for unionized positions relative to nonunionized ones; however, the differences are not statistically significant. In addition, although the raw data indicate that the investments in intensive search among business units in the sample are, in fact, greater for union over nonunion positions, nor are these differences statistically significant.

      For both measures of extensive search, Table 2.4 indicates that employers invest nominally, but not significantly more, when hiring for nonunion over union positions. Whereas, on average, firms in the sample interview five candidates per hire for unionized positions, they interview six candidates per hire for employees in nonunionized positions.

Likewise, the number of regularly used recruiting sources for nonunion vacancies is slightly (but not significantly) more than the number used on a regular basis for positions covered by collective bargaining.[11]

The raw numbers in Table 2.4 also suggest that there is more intensive search by employers for union workers over nonunion workers in the same jobs. There are, however, no statistically significant differences exhibited by business lines in this sample. The data show that applicants for jobs covered by collective bargaining are only nominally subjected to more pre-employment selection tests[12] than applicants for nonunion jobs and again, only nominally more likely to be recruited from an informal source than applicants for nonunion jobs.

In sum, the data demonstrate that there is substantial variation in employers' investments in both extensive and intensive search strategies. The data also suggest that there are differences in of recruitment firms' usage and selection methods for locating and hiring different types of workers; although the hypotheses regarding

TABLE 2.4

*Mean Usage of Recruitment and Selection Procedures by Business Units in the Sample for Union and Nonunion Workers*

|  | Union Workers[a] | | Nonunion Workers[a] | |
| --- | --- | --- | --- | --- |
|  | Mean Percent Usage | N | Mean Percent Usage | N |
| Extensive Search Mean Interviews per Hire | 5.08 | 151 | 5.67 | 466 |
| Number of Recruiting Sources Used | 3.82 | 175 | 4.84 | 490 |
| Intensive Search Number of Selection Tests Given | 1.95 | 174 | 1.23 | 487 |
| Percent of Informal Recruiting Sources Used | 0.47 | 167 | 0.40 | 488 |

[a] Both Union and Nonunion categories include professional, technical, clerical, production and manufacturing workers.

differences in investment for high and low-level employees, and union and nonunion workers were not supported statistically in simple statistical tests which do not control for the effects of other factors hypothesized to affect recruitment and selection investment decisions. In order to improve our understanding of the hiring process, the factors underlying the variation in employers' recruitment and selection strategies will be examined next. Subsequent to an analysis of the determinants of the firm's recruitment and selection strategies, the effects they have on the performance of the workforce will be explored.

In the next chapter, a theoretical framework that can be used to investigate the determinants of the firm's choice of recruitment and selection strategies is presented and the results of the empirical analysis using this framework are also reported.

## NOTES

1. For details, see Delaney, Lewin and Ichniowski 1989, and Delaney, Ichniowski and Lewin 1989. This survey will henceforth be referred to as the Columbia HR Survey.

2. See Appendix for further description and discussion of the database used in this dissertation.

3. This is a limitation in using the Compustat II data for longitudinal studies; another is that firms that go out of business are dropped from the sample entirely (i.e., their histories are purged from files for past years).

4. Technically, the unit of analysis in this study is the *business unit*. The terms *firm* and *organization* will be used interchangeably with *business unit* throughout the book, however. Strictly speaking, when I speak of a firm or an organization, I am referring to a single line of business within the firm or organization.

5. The Employee Polygraph Protection Act of 1988, which prohibits the use of polygraphs for making employment decisions, was passed *after* the data were collected and the analyses in this book were conducted. Today, a similar study would not include polygraphs among an employer's choice of selection tests to screen job applicants.

6. The high-level job category includes managers, professional and technical workers; the low-level job category includes clericals, and manufacturing and production workers.

7. In difference-in-proportions tests, none of the differences in Table 2.3 was found to be statistically significant.

8. When disaggregated, it can be noted that the sources used relatively more for low-level jobs are all virtually costless to the organization, whereas those used more for the high-level jobs are much more expensive, as was hypothesized. Newspaper advertisements, both undergraduate and, graduate schools, search firms, and private employment agencies are the recruiting sources used significantly more often for high-level jobs. In contrast, government employment agencies, employee referrals, walk-ins, and promotion-from-within are more frequently employed as recruiting sources for low-level jobs.

9. In this study, search firms are overwhelmingly preferred for the recruitment of managers; seventy-five percent of the firms use them, while the next closest category for which search firms are a widely used recruiting source is nonunion professional or technical workers at forty-six percent.

10. However, there are no statistically significant differences in the use of polygraphs, drug tests or physical examination between low and high-level workers.

11. To investigate the union-nonunion difference more closely, each recruiting source was analyzed individually for statistically significant differences in union-nonunion use. For nonunion workers, the recruiting sources used significantly more frequently include: newspaper advertisements, college recruiting, search firms, private employment agencies, employee referrals, and walk-ins. In fact, there are no recruiting sources that are used significantly more often for union job titles than for nonunion job titles. The magnitude of the differences in the union-nonunion comparison is much greater in most cases than in the high-low job level comparisons; for instance, on average, only six percent of the business units in the sample use search firms to recruit union workers, whereas almost forty-seven percent of them do for nonunion workers. Likewise, less than twenty percent of the firms recruit at undergraduate (19.9 percent) and graduate (14.1 percent) schools for workers in unionized jobs; whereas, 63.6 percent of the firms reported recruiting nonunion workers at undergraduate institutions and 51.2 percent at graduate or professional schools.

12. When selection test usage is examined separately for union-nonunion differences, the following was found. Skill tests are required of job candidates in the nonunion category significantly more often than in the union category (65 percent and 45.6 percent respectively). Furthermore, candidates for unionized jobs are required to take both drug tests and physical exams significantly more often than job candidates for nonunion jobs. Again, the magnitude of the difference is large—49 percent of the firms report using drug tests for their union job candidates as opposed to 26 percent for their nonunion job candidates; likewise, over 76 percent of the business units require job candidates for unionized positions to have a physical exam prior to employment, while 45 percent require it of applicants for nonunion jobs.

# CHAPTER THREE

# The Determinants of a Firm's Recruitment and Selection Strategies

As was established in the last chapter, there is great variation in the recruitment and selection strategies used by United States firms. In an effort to increase our understanding of the variation in the hiring process, this chapter explores which factors influence a firm's choice of recruitment and selection strategies.

In this chapter, I shall first specify an empirical model for testing the hypotheses generated by the theoretical framework from Chapter One concerning the determinants of a firm's recruitment and selection strategies. The results of the estimated models will be presented and discussed in the subsequent section. Recall that the hypotheses from Chapter One are: (1) Extensive search, as measured by (a) the number of interviews per hire and (b) the number of recruiting sources used, is expected to be positively influenced by firm size, the percentage of high-level workers in the firm, the extent to which the firm values its employees, the percentages of whites and males and the education level of individuals in the labor force from which the firm hires, and the amount of its capital expenditures, and negatively influenced by the extent of unionization of the firm. (2) Intensive search, as captured by (c) the number of selection tests administered and (d) a preference for informal over formal recruiting sources, is expected to be positively influenced by firm size, the extent of unionization of the firm (for (c) only), the extent to which the firm values its employees, the percentages of whites and males and the education level of individuals in the labor force from which it hires, and the amount of its capital expenditures, and negatively by the percentage of high-level workers in the firm and the extent of unionization of the firm (for (d) only). (3) It is hypothesized that firms will increase their formal planning and evaluation of hiring policies with increases in firm size, the extent of unionization of the firm, the extent to which they value their employees, the percentages of whites and males and the education level of individuals in the labor force from which they hire, the percentage of high-level workers in the firm, and the amount of their capital expenditures.

## SECTION A: MODELING the DETERMINANTS of a FIRM'S RECRUITMENT and SELECTION METHODS

In this section, I shall present an empirical model for investigating factors that influence a firm's decision to use various recruitment and selection practices, and discuss the operationalization of variables in the model. The last part of this section contains the model to be estimated and the estimation techniques to be used.

A firm's choice of recruitment and selection strategy depends on specific firm characteristics, its industry, and the labor markets from which it hires. In this study, I focus on factors that influence six particular decisions the firm faces when setting its recruitment and selection strategies. These are the dependent variables of the determinants model and they are described below.

*Dependent Variables.* Two administrative practices are the first to be investigated. They are, (a) whether to engage in formal human resource planning for recruitment and selection, and (b), whether to carry out formal, regular evaluation of the recruitment and selection functions.

In the Columbia HR survey, firms were asked whether they engaged in formal human resource planning for staffing. The response to this question was coded as a dichotomous yes-no variable called HRPLAN in the model. HRPLAN equals one if the firm has a formal, written HR plan for selection and staffing, and zero if not.

The other firm-wide, administrative practice to be used as a dependent variable in this study is the firm's choice to engage in formal evaluation of its hiring policies. As a dependent measure, this policy variable is measured as a firm-wide dummy, called RSEVAL.

RSEVAL takes on the value one, if the firm practices formal evaluation of its recruitment and selection policies and zero, if not. Data for this variable were also obtained from the Columbia HR survey.

Employer extensive search is represented by two variables; the first is the number of selection interviews administered per hire. INTRVS is the variable name and it is equal to the number of interviews per hire the firm administers to job candidates in each of the seven job categories, weighted by the percent of workers in the category and then summed over the seven categories. The second measure of extensive search is given by the sum of the weighted number of recruiting sources that the firm regularly uses to produce job candidates;[1] the variable name given to it is SOURCES. As developed in Chapter One, firms invest in extensive search as a means of gathering more information about the labor market prior to making hiring decisions. Investments in extensive search are hypothesized to improve the quality of the firm's workforce.

The other type of employer search of interest in this volume is employer intensive search. Intensive search is the employer's effort to gather more information about each applicant in the pool prior to making employment decisions. Two measures of intensive search are also used as dependent variables in the determinants model. The first of these, TESTS, equals the sum of the weighted number of pre-employment selection tests regularly used by the firm to screen job applicants. The selection tests inquired about in the survey include ability tests, skill tests, polygraphs, drug tests and physical examinations. The second measure of intensive search is represented by the extent to which the employer prefers informal recruiting sources to formal ones. PCTINFML is the name of the latter measure of intensive search and its value equals the sum of the weighted percent of the firm's regularly used recruiting sources for each of the seven worker categories previously described that are informal. The recruiting sources referred to as "informal" in this measure include employee referrals and internal candidates (or promotions-from-within). Formal recruiting sources include: newspaper advertisements, undergraduate college recruiting, graduate or professional school recruiting, search firms, direct applicants,[2] government employment agencies, and private employment agencies.

In summary, six recruitment and selection strategy choices are of interest in this study. They, and their variable names, are (1) whether or not to formally plan for recruitment and selection (HRPLAN), (2) whether or not to regularly evaluate the staffing process (RSEVAL), (3) the number of interviews per hire to conduct (INTRVS), (4) the number of recruiting sources to use to generate applicants (SOURCES), (5) the number of pre-employment selection tests to administer to job applicants (TESTS), and (6) the preference for use of informal versus formal recruiting sources (PCTINFML).

TABLE 3.1

*Dependent Variables of the Determinants Model*

| Variable Name | Definition |
|---|---|
| Administrative Policies<br>HRPLAN | Equals one if business unit engages in formal HR Planning for Staffing and Selection. |
| RSEVAL | Equals one if business unit engages in formal Evaluation of Staffing and Selection Policy. |
| Extensive Search<br>INTRVS | Number of interviews administered per hire[a] |
| SOURCES<br>Intensive Search | Number of regularly used recruiting sources[a] |
| TESTS | Number of selection tests regularly administered to applicants[a,b] |
| PCTINFML | Percentage of recruiting sources that are informal[a,c] |

[a] This variable is measured for workers in each of seven categories in 1986 (managers, union and nonunion professional and technical workers, union and nonunion clericals, and union and nonunion manufacturing workers), weighted by the percent of workers in the respective category, and then summed over the seven categories.
[b] Selection tests include: ability tests, skill tests, polygraphs, drug tests and physical examinations.
[c] Informal recruiting sources include: employee referrals and in-house candidates; formal recruiting sources include: newspaper advertisements, undergraduate institutions, graduate and professional institutions, direct applicants, private and public employment agencies, and search firms.

Table 3.1 presents a complete list of the dependent variables to be used in the determinants model. We turn now to the factors hypothesized to affect employer search strategies.

*Independent Variables.* As developed in the theoretical model of Chapter One, the factors likely to influence a firm's use of the aforementioned recruitment and selection practices include firm-specific factors, characteristics of the industry, and labor-market factors. How each factor is operationalized in the empirical model is discussed in this section.

  *Firm-specific Factors.* The first of the firm-specific explanatory variables is the firm's size. Large firms are hypothesized to invest relatively more than small firms in search by planning and evaluating the recruitment and selection strategies as well as by engaging in extensive and intensive search. In this study, firm size is measured by the number of employees in the firm and the variable is called SIZE. The coefficient on SIZE for the reasons outlined in Chapter One is expected to be positive.

  Due to the higher average wages and the longer expected tenure of unionized workers, the extent of unionization of the firm's workforce leads the firm to invest more in both extensive and intensive search. However, as was discussed in Chapter One, certain institutional factors affecting hiring practices that stem from collective bargaining agreements may dominate these effects of unionism on certain measures of search strategies. In particular, it is expected that the number of recruiting sources (SOURCES), the number of interviews conducted per hire (INTRVS), and the preference for informal recruiting sources (PCTINFML) may be negatively affected by the extent of unionism in the firm. Unionization (UNION) is measured in this study by the percent of employees covered by a written collective bargaining agreement. The coefficient on UNION in the equation using TESTS and PCTINFML as the dependent variable is expected to be greater than zero. Data for this variable were obtained from the Columbia HR survey.

  PCTHIGH is the name of the variable used to measure the percentage of high-level workers in the firm. The value of PCTHIGH is equal to the number of high-level employees (*i.e.*, managers, professionals and technical workers) divided by the total number of workers in the firm. The sign on the coefficient of PCTHIGH is expected to be greater than zero in equations using each of the six dependent variables measures with the exception of TESTS and PCTINFML, where it is expected to have a negative effect.

The extent to which the firm values its employees, is expected to have an effect on the firm's hiring policies. As discussed in Chapter One, a firm's attitude towards its employees may be captured by the degree of employee involvement or participation. The firm that highly values its employees has been hypothesized to engage in both the formal planning and evaluation of the recruitment and selection functions. Likewise, it is expected that the number of interviews per hire will increase with the degree to which a firm values its workers. In this study, the degree to which a firm values its employees is measured by an index that contains the answers to twelve survey questions designed to tap the extent of employee involvement in the organization. These questions and how they were scored are shown in the Appendix. The score on the variable VALUES is the sum of the answers to twelve questions contained in the index. A high score on VALUES reflects a high degree of employee participation in the firm, or, a willingness to share authority with employees. The coefficient on VALUES is expected to be greater than zero in equations using all measures of recruitment and selection strategies as dependent variables.

It is expected that firms providing relatively more training will also invest more in the hiring process via increased extensive and intensive search and formal planning and evaluation of the recruitment and selection functions. In the equations to be estimated, the value that the variable TRAINING takes on is equal to the percent of employee groups to which formal training is provided by the employer.[3]

Increased capital expenditures per employee predict greater average expected values of labor services. It was hypothesized in Chapter One that there are relatively greater gains to extensive and intensive search for employers who invest heavily in capital equipment. A measure of the business unit's capital per employee also captures the effects of the firm's technology on its hiring practices. For these reasons, it is expected that the coefficient on KEXP—a variable that equals the firm's capital expenditures in millions of dollars standardized by workforce size[4]—will be greater than zero. Data for KEXP come from the Compustat II Industry Segment files for 1986.

*Industry Characteristics.* The hiring process and firms' investments in recruitment and selection are likely to differ by industry. There are certain hiring standards, characteristic pay structures and traditional approaches to hiring that vary from industry to industry. Dummy variables are included in the model to capture these differences. These variables include the following groupings of two-digit SIC industrial groups: (1) agriculture, mining and construction (AGMNCO), (2) wholesale and retail trade (TRADE), (3) transportation (TRAN), (4) finance, insurance and real estate (FIRE), and (5) the service industry (SERV). The excluded industrial group in the regression analyses is manufacturing (MANU).

*Labor-Market Factors.* The final category of determinants includes characteristics of the labor markets from which the firm hires. It was stated in Chapter One that because of legislation affecting the hiring process, the composition of the labor market, in terms of the characteristics which are protected by law, will have an impact on the firm's recruitment and selection strategies. Two labor market factors, in particular, are expected to influence the firm's choice of recruiting and selection methods—the percentage of male workers and the percentage of white workers in the labor market from which the firm hires. It was hypothesized that firms hiring from labor markets with a high percentage male (or white) workers will be more likely to engage in HR planning and the formal evaluation of staffing policies. It was likewise hypothesized that all measures of extensive and intensive search will increase with both the percentage male and the percentage white in the firm's labor market.

The variables used in this study to measure the percentage of males and whites in the labor market from which the business unit recruits and hires come from the Current Population Survey (CPS) data for 1985 and are called PCTMALE and PCTWHITE respectively. These variables measure the percentage of male and white workers in the firm's *industry* respectively. These measures were included in the study in order to capture the hypothesized effects of labor market characteristics described above.[5] Unfortunately, there is a potential problem with these measures. That is, they are not very precise measures of the labor market that the firm faces when hiring. Preferable measures would be the percentage male and white of workers in the *geographic* area from which the firm recruits and selects applicants for hire. However, most of the firms in this sample have multiple establishments that may be located in different geographic regions, and data were not collected about the precise geographic location of each. Therefore, more accurate measures of the actual labor market from which the business unit hires are not available. Because of the imprecision of the measures, the effects of labor market characteristics might not be detected in the analyses.

The same problem arises in the variable used to capture the mean level of education among workers in the labor market from which the firm hires. Recall that it was hypothesized in Chapter One that the employer will search more at both the extensive and intensive margins, as well as have a greater chance of formally planning and evaluating hiring policies, as the mean level of education of individuals in the labor market rises.[6] MGRADE is the name of the variable used to measure educational attainment, and it equals the mean years of education completed among workers in the business line's four-digit SIC industry. These data were obtained from the 1985 Current Population Survey. MGRADE is expected to have a positive coefficient in the estimated equations.

A complete list of the explanatory variables to be used in the determinants model and their definitions are presented and defined in Table 3.2.

*Equations and Estimation Techniques for the Determinants Model.* In summary, the following model of the determinants of the firm's recruitment and selection strategies whose variables are defined above may be estimated:

$$
\begin{aligned}
\text{HRPLAN} &= \beta_0 c + \beta_1 \text{SIZE} + \beta_2 \text{UNION} + \beta_3 \text{PCTHIGH} + \beta_4 \text{VALUES} + \\
\text{RSEVAL} & \\
\text{INTRVS} & \quad \beta_5 \text{TRAINING} + \beta_6 \text{KEXP} + \beta_7 \text{FIRE} + \beta_8 \text{TRADE} + \beta_9 \text{TRAN} + \\
\text{SOURCES} & \\
\text{TESTS} & \quad \beta \text{SERV} + \beta_{11} \text{AGMNCO} + \beta_{12} \text{PCTWHITE} + \beta_{13} \text{PCTMALE} + \\
\text{PCTINFML} & \\
& \quad \beta_{14} \text{MGRADE} + \varepsilon
\end{aligned}
$$

The error term is represented by $\varepsilon$ and is assumed to be randomly distributed with a mean of zero and constant variance. This model allows us to observe the existence of and extent to which the given characteristics determine an organization's choice of recruitment and selection practices.

TABLE 3.2

*Independent Variables in the Determinants Model*

| Variable Name | Definition |
|---|---|
| SIZE | Total Number of Employees in the Firm |
| UNION | Percent of Employees covered by Collective Bargaining |
| PCTHIGH | Percent of high-level employees |
| VALUES | Score on Values Index[a] |
| TRAINING | Percent of employee groups to whom formal training is offered |
| KEXP | Capital expenditures in millions of dollars divided by the number of employees. |
| FIRE | Equals one if firm is in finance, insurance or real estate industry. |
| AGMNCO | Equals one if firm is in agriculture, mining or construction industry. |
| MANU[b] | Equals one if firm is in manufacturing industry. |
| TRAN | Equals one if firm is in transportation industry. |
| TRADE | Equals one if firm is in wholesale or retail trade industry. |
| SERV | Equals one if firm is in service industry. |
| PCTMALE | Percent of male employees in the firm's 4-digit SIC industry in 1985 |
| PCTWHITE | Percent of white employees in the firm's 4-digit SIC industry in 1985 |
| MGRADE | Mean highest grade completed in firm's 4-digit SIC industry in 1985 |

[a]See Appendix for construction of Values Index.
[b]This is the excluded industrial group in the regression analysis.

The first two dependent variables listed in the determinants model above, HRPLAN and RSEVAL, are measured at the firm level; that is, in the survey it was asked if the firm engages in formal human resource planning for staffing and selection (YES or NO) and if it formally evaluates its selection and staffing policies (YES or NO). The values that HRPLAN and RSEVAL can assume are one (for YES) and zero (for NO) only. As a result, maximum likelihood estimation is used in lieu of ordinary least squares regression (Maddala 1977) to estimate the model for these measures of the dependent variable. The results of maximum likelihood estimation will indicate the existence and extent of the effects of the specified independent variables on the probability of the firm's use of these two administrative practices concerning the hiring process.

The model is estimated using the ordinary least squares (OLS) for the remaining dependent variable measures (*i.e.*, the number of interviews per hire (INTRVS), the number of recruiting sources (SOURCES), the percent of informal recruiting sources used (PCTINFML), and the number of selection tests (TESTS)). The results of the determinants model analyses are reported in the next section.

## SECTION B: EMPIRICAL FINDINGS and DISCUSSION

Table 3.3 gives the average values of the independent variables in the model. There are a total of 495 business units included in the study. The sample encompasses relatively large business units, with a mean size of 6082 employees and a median of 767. The range is from 2 to 238,000 employees.

Approximately forty percent (n=170) of the business units in the sample have no unionized employees. On average, eighteen percent of the business units' workers are covered by collective bargaining.

The bulk of firms in the sample are in the manufacturing sector (46.5 percent); the next largest group is in the transportation industry (16.2 percent). The least represented industrial group is agriculture, mining and construction (6.5 percent). Firms from the financial, insurance and real estate industries, and from the service industries account for approximately twelve percent each.

The mean value of the VALUES index for the sample is 27. Recall that the VALUES index attempts to capture the extent to which the firm values its employees and is willing to share decision making and other types of authority with them.[7] The VALUES index ranges from a minimum of zero to a maximum of 60. Approximately sixty-eight percent of the sample firms have measures on the VALUES index of between 18 and 36.

The TRAINING variables captures the percentage of worker groups to which formal training programs are available within the business unit. The TRAINING variable has a mean value for business lines in the sample of 40 percent. The mean value of TRAINING says that, on average, business units in the sample offer formal training to forty percent of all worker groups.[8]

TABLE 3.3

*Mean Values for Variables in Determinants Model (Standard Deviation = SD)*

| Variable | Mean | SD |
|---|---|---|
| Measure of Recruitment and Selection Strategy | | |
| HR Planning (HRPLAN) | 0.419 | 0.494 |
| R&S Evaluation (RSEVAL) | 0.857 | 0.351 |
| Interviews/Hire (INTRVS) | 5.224 | 4.408 |
| Recruiting Sources (SOURCES) | 4.442 | 1.445 |
| Number of Selection Tests (TESTS) | 1.180 | 1.067 |
| Percent Informal Sources (PCTINFML) | 0.396 | 0.130 |
| Explanatory Variables | | |
| Number of Employees (SIZE) | 6082.140 | 18853.200 |
| Percent Unionized (UNION) | 0.181 | 0.266 |
| Percent High-Level Employees (PCTHIGH) | 0.389 | 0.222 |
| Hiring Policy Values (VALUES) | 27.008 | 8.914 |
| Percent of Worker Groups with Formal | | |
| Training Programs (TRAINING) | 0.403 | 0.414 |
| Capital Expenditures per Employee (KEXP) | 0.061 | 0.345 |
| (in millions of dollars) | | |
| Industry | | |
| Agric/Mining/Construction (AGMNCO) | 0.065 | 0.246 |
| Finance/Insurance/R. Estate (FIRE) | 0.119 | 0.324 |
| Manufacturing (MANU) | 0.465 | 0.499 |
| Trade (TRADE) | 0.075 | 0.263 |
| Transportation (TRAN) | 0.162 | 0.368 |
| Service (SERV) | 0.115 | 0.320 |
| In Firm's Industry | | |
| Mean Highest Grade Completed (MGRADE) | 13.962 | 0.916 |
| Percent Male (PCTMALE) | 63.849 | 16.535 |
| Percent White (PCTWHITE) | 89.495 | 4.767 |

NB: Total number of firms in sample=495

The average firm's capital expenditures in 1986 totalled 92.5 million dollars. KEXP, the variable measuring capital expenditures per employee, ranged in value from zero to 4.18 million dollars per employee, with a mean value of $60,732 per employee. The large values of KEXP are a reflection of the size of business units in the sample.

I turn now to the investigation of factors that affect a firm's investment in recruitment and selection strategies.

*Formal Human Resource Planning and Evaluation of Recruitment and Selection.* The first recruitment and selection strategies to be analyzed are the firm's decisions of whether or not to engage in both the formal planning for staffing and the evaluation of hiring practices. The findings regarding the determinants of these policy decisions are given in Table 3.4 and Table 3.5 respectively. The dependent variables are measured dichotomously and they equal one if the firm engages in planning and formally evaluates its recruitment and selection policies, and zero if not.

Before discussing the results, an explanation of the column headed "$\partial P/\partial X$" in Tables 3.4 and 3.5 is called for. Due to the dichotomous nature of the dependent variable, linear regression analysis is inappropriate to use (Maddala 1983). Thus, the model is specified as a logit probability function and estimated with the maximum likelihood technique as described by McFadden (1980). Unfortunately, unlike those in a linear probability model, the coefficients in a non-linear logit equation are not conducive to intuitive interpretation. Specifically, the change in probability caused by a one unit change in a given independent variable depends upon the values of the other independent variables. By taking the derivative of the estimated probability with respect to each of the independent variables (*i.e.,* $\partial P/\partial X$) at the average value of each, we can interpret the number in this column as the effect of a one-unit change in the independent variable on the probability that the firm will engage in formal planning for recruitment and selection or formal evaluation of the staffing function.[9]

The results reported in Table 3.4 indicate that a number of firm specific factors predominate in the firm's decision to invest in HR planning for staffing and selection. In particular, the size of the firm, the extent to which employees are involved in the management of the

## TABLE 3.4

*The Determinants of HR Planning for Recruitment and Selection*
*(standard deviations in parentheses)*

| Explanatory Variable | $\beta$ | $\dfrac{\partial P^{a}}{\partial X}$ |
|---|---|---|
| Dependent Variable = Probability that the firm engages in HR Planning for Selection and Staffing | | |
| Constant | -3.291 | -0.806 |
| | (2.887) | |
| SIZE | 0.267E-04 *** | 0.653E-05 |
| | (0.116E-04) | |
| UNION | 1.375 *** | 0.337 |
| | (0.555) | |
| PCTHIGH | 0.317 | 0.776E-01 |
| | (0.615) | |
| VALUES | 0.308E-01 ** | 0.753E-02 |
| | (0.146E-01) | |
| TRAINING | 1.595 **** | 0.391 |
| | (0.320) | |
| KEXP | 0.415 | 0.102 |
| | (0.452) | |
| FINANCE | -0.848E-01 | -0.208E-01 |
| | (0.488) | |
| AGMNCO | 0.381E-01 | 0.933E-02 |
| | (0.492) | |
| TRADE | -0.286 | -0.700E-01 |
| | (0.504) | |
| TRANSPORT | -0.773 ** | -0.189 |
| | (0.379) | |
| SERVICE | -0.110 | -0.270E-01 |
| | (0.426) | |
| MGRADE | 0.354E-01 | 0.867E-02 |
| | (0.174) | |
| PCTMALE | -0.634E-02 | -0.155E-02 |
| | (0.933E-02) | |
| PCTWHITE | 0.120E-01 | 0.295E-02 |
| | (0.279E-01) | |
| Adjusted-$R^{2}$ [b] | .01 | |
| Chi-Square | 1.92 | |
| Sample Size | 384 | |

**** = $p < .01$; *** = $p < .025$; ** = $p < .05$; * = $p < .10$ (two-tailed tests). The excluded industrial group is manufacturing.

[a] - for description see text
[b] - from Aldrich and Nelson, 1984, p.57.

business, the amount of formal training the firm makes available to various worker groups, and the extent to which the firm is unionized, all positively and significantly affect the probability that the firm will have a formal, written HR plan for staffing. The extent of formal training in the firm has the strongest effect—increasing by one the number of occupations to whom formal training is available, increases the probability that the firm will have a formal, written HR plan for selection and staffing by approximately 39 percentage points. The effect of unionism is also relatively strong (34 percentage points). Although also positive and significant, the effects of the variables VALUES and SIZE are much smaller, relative to those of training and unionization.

The only statistically significant industry effect is the negative likelihood that transportation firms will engage in HR planning as compared to manufacturing firms. Among labor-market factors, although none is statistically significant in effect, the variables MGRADE and PCTWHITE both have positive signs. PCTMALE has a negative (albeit not significant) coefficient, contrary to the predicted effect.

The results of the logit analysis suggest that firm-specific factors are relatively more important than industry or labor-market factors in predicting whether or not a firm will invest in HR planning for recruitment and selection.

Looking at the determinants of the probability that the firm will formally evaluate its hiring policies (see Table 3.5), some firm-specific, industry group and labor-market factors all appear to have significant effects. As was the case for the determinants of HR planning, the extent of available formal training for employees has a positive and highly significant effect on formal recruitment and selection evaluation: making training available to each additional group of workers increases the probability of formal hiring policy evaluation by approximately twenty percent.

As for industry effects, firms in finance, insurance and real estate, agriculture, mining and construction, and the transportation industries are all significantly less likely than firms in the manufacturing industry to formally evaluate their recruitment and selection strategies. The financial services industrial group effect is the greatest of the three: being in the finance, insurance or real estate industry (as opposed to manufacturing), decreases the probability of

TABLE 3.5

*The Determinants of the Formal Evaluation of Recruitment and Selection Policies*
*(standard deviations in parentheses)*

| Explanatory Variable | $\beta$ | $\dfrac{\partial P^a}{\partial X}$ |
|---|---|---|
| Dependent Variable = Probability that the firm engages in Formal Evaluation of Staffing Policies | | |
| Constant | -4.774 | -0.280 |
| | (4.398) | |
| SIZE | 0.394E-04 | 0.231E-05 |
| | (0.415E-04) | |
| UNION | 0.835 | 0.490E-01 |
| | (0.820) | |
| PCTHIGH | 1.332 | 0.781E-01 |
| | (1.017) | |
| VALUES | -0.183E-01 | -0.107E-02 |
| | (0.222E-01) | |
| TRAINING | 3.385 **** | 0.199 |
| | (0.700) | |
| KEXP | 0.782 | 0.459E-01 |
| | (1.587) | |
| FINANCE | -2.284 **** | -0.134 |
| | (0.769) | |
| AGMNCO | -1.169 * | -0.686E-01 |
| | (0.718) | |
| TRADE | -0.123 | -0.721E-02 |
| | (0.745) | |
| TRANSPORT | -0.839 * | -0.492E-01 |
| | (0.553) | |
| SERVICE | 1.077 | 0.632E-01 |
| | (1.088) | |
| MGRADE | 0.377 * | 0.221E-01 |
| | (0.262) | |
| PCTMALE | -0.646E-02 | -0.379E-03 |
| | (0.151E-01) | |
| PCTWHITE | 0.114E-01 | 0.667E-03 |
| | (0.410E-01) | |

| | |
|---|---|
| Adjusted-$R^{2b}$ | .01 |
| Chi-Square | 4.39 * |
| Sample Size | 337 |

**** = p < .01; *** = p < .025; ** = p < .05; * = p < .10 (two-tailed tests). The excluded industrial group is manufacturing.

[a] - for description see text
[b] - from Aldrich and Nelson, 1984, p.57.

doing formal program evaluation of recruitment and selection policies by over thirteen percentage points. None of the industry effects is larger than the effects of TRAINING, suggesting a greater influence of this firm-specific factor over industry specific factors in the firm's decision to practice formal and regular evaluation of its hiring strategies.

Finally, the average industry education level (MGRADE) has a positive and significant impact on probability of evaluation (approximately a two percentage point increase in the likelihood to engage in formal recruitment and selection evaluation for each additional year of education for workers in the firm's industry).

In sum, the firm's investment in search as captured by the administrative policy of formally and regularly evaluating its hiring strategy appears to be affected by factors both in the firm itself and in the environment in which it works. The more "proactive" administrative practice of HR planning appears to depend relatively more upon firm specific characteristics; whereas the more "reactive" administrative practice of formally and regularly evaluating staffing policies seems to depend upon which industry the firm is in and conditions of the labor market in which the firm operates in addition to firm-specific factors.

*Extensive Search.* Firms increase the extensiveness of search for workers by increasing the number of candidates screened per hire (Rees 1966), as well as by increasing the number of regularly used recruiting sources (Malm 1954). As discussed in Chapter One, increasing extensive search is hypothesized to improve the employment match and subsequent employee performance by providing the employer with more information about the applicant pool prior to making decisions to hire (Barron and Bishop 1985). In Tables 3.6 and 3.7, we observe significant differences in the factors which influence the firms investment in extensive search as measured by the number of interviews per hire and the number of regularly used recruiting sources as well.

*Interviews per Hire.* Table 3.6 reports the results of the effects of the hypothesized determinants on employer extensive search as measured by the number of interviews per hire. As was the case with

HR planning, firm-specific factors appear to have the greatest influence on this measure of extensive search.

The first firm-specific factor that significantly influences the number of interviews per hire the firm conducts is the degree to which the firm is unionized. As was hypothesized, the effect of unionization

TABLE 3.6

*The Determinants of the Firm's Choice of Number of Interviews per Hire to Conduct*

| Explanatory Variable | Dependent Variable = INTRVS | |
|---|---|---|
| | $\beta$ | Standard Deviation |
| Constant | 2.632 | 5.818 |
| SIZE | 0.244E-05 | 0.122E-04 |
| UNION | -1.928 * | 1.085 |
| PCTHIGH | 0.720 | 1.239 |
| VALUES | 0.441E-01 | 0.285E-01 |
| TRAINING | 0.228 | 0.624 |
| KEXP | 2.200 **** | 0.673 |
| FIRE | -0.941 | 0.983 |
| AGMNCO | 0.188E-01 | 0.982 |
| TRADE | 1.536 | 0.984 |
| TRANSPRT | 1.248 * | 0.734 |
| SERVICE | -0.539 | 0.872 |
| MGRADE | 0.255 | 0.340 |
| PCTMALE | -0.633E-02 | 0.184E-01 |
| PCTWHITE | -0.229E-01 | 0.555E-01 |

| | |
|---|---|
| Adjusted-$R^2$ | .04 |
| F-Statistic | 2.033 *** |
| Sample Size | 380 |

**** = $p < .01$; *** = $p < .025$; ** = $p < .05$; * = $p < .10$ (two-tailed tests); excluded industry is manufacturing.

is to significantly decrease the number of interviews conducted by the firm per hire. Specifically, for each percent increase in collective bargaining coverage of workers, there is an decrease of approximately one interview per hire. Given that the average number of interviews conducted per hire is slightly over five, the union effect is considerable. As was discussed above, firms with unionized workers may have collective bargaining agreements that contain seniority clauses or that may specify that unionized jobs must be filled from a list of employees or applicants who took a test, in the order of test scores. Because of the existence of rules that dictate who will fill the available job, in cases like these, fewer interviews per hire are necessary.

The other firm-specific factor significantly likely to increase the number of interviews per hire is the amount of the firm's capital expenditures per employee. As predicted, the more capital equipment the prospective employee will have to work with, the more information the employer will collect prior to making hiring decisions. Significantly more extensive search, as measured by interviews per hire, occurs in firms with large amounts of capital expenditures per worker.

There is little significant evidence of the effects of labor-market factors or industry characteristics in the firm's choice of the number of interviews per hire to conduct. Namely, business units in the transportation industry appear to search significantly more at the extensive margin by means of conducting more interviews per hire than those in the excluded group (*i.e.*, manufacturing); specifically, firms in the transportation industry conduct close to one more interview per hire than those in manufacturing. Other industry effects are not statistically different from zero. Further, while the effect of education level on extensive search is positive, the signs on the coefficients of variables representing the percentages of males and whites in the industry are negative, which is contrary to what was expected.

*Number of Recruiting Sources Used.* The results of the estimation when the number of regularly used recruiting sources (*i.e.*, SOURCES) is used as the dependent variable to measure extensive search indicate that many of the firm and industry specific factors have a significant effect on extensive search. The results of the analysis are given in Table 3.7. Twenty percent of the variance is explained by the model and six of the thirteen explanatory variables are significant at the ten percent level or better.

TABLE 3.7

*The Determinants of the Firm's Choice of Number of Recruiting Sources to Use*

| Explanatory Variable | Dependent Variable = SOURCES | |
| --- | --- | --- |
| | $\beta$ | Standard Deviation |
| Constant | 1.211 | 1.665 |
| SIZE | 0.512E-05 | 0.349E-05 |
| UNION | -1.300 **** | 0.311 |
| PCTHIGH | 0.932 **** | 0.355 |
| VALUES | 0.113E-01 | 0.816E-02 |
| TRAINING | 0.562 **** | 0.179 |
| KEXP | -0.135E-01 | 0.193 |
| FIRE | -0.422 | 0.281 |
| AGMNCO | -1.641 **** | 0.281 |
| TRADE | -0.288 | 0.282 |
| TRANSPRT | -0.379 * | 0.210 |
| SERVICE | -0.448 * | 0.250 |
| MGRADE | 0.470E-01 | 0.972E-01 |
| PCTMALE | 0.952E-03 | 0.527E-02 |
| PCTWHITE | 0.238E-01 | 0.159E-01 |
| Adjusted-$R^2$ | .20 | |
| F-Statistic | 7.679 **** | |
| Sample Size | 380 | |

**** = $p < .01$; *** = $p < .025$; ** = $p < .05$; * = $p < .10$ (two-tailed tests); excluded industry is manufacturing.

The industry effects are all negative. Business units in agriculture, mining and construction, transportation and the services industries all use significantly fewer recruiting sources than those in the manufacturing industry. As compared with firms in manufacturing, firms in these industries invest less in extensive search by virtue of using approximately one less recruiting sources regularly.[10] The negative effect is largest for firms in the agriculture, mining and construction category—these use close to two fewer recruiting sources than manufacturing firms.

Among the firm-specific factors, UNION has the greatest significant effect, and as in the case of interviews per hire, its effect is negative. Thus, for both measures of extensive search it appears that unionization significantly reduces employer extensive search. Among other firm-specific factors, the percent of high-level workers, and the extent to which the firm makes formal training available to different groups of employees both have positive and significant effects on the number of recruiting sources the firm will use. The effects are rather small (*i.e.*, a one unit increase in the values of each of these variables causes an increase of less than one recruiting source). The effects of these firm-specific factors all support the proposed hypotheses.

In sum, we find that firm-specific factors appear to be the main determinants of employer investment in extensive search. Capital expenditures per employee positively influence extensive search as captured by the number of interviews administered per hire. Extensive search as measured by the number of recruiting sources regularly used is positively and significantly influenced by both the percent of high level workers in the firm and the extent to which formal training is available to workers. And, as predicted, both measures of extensive search are negatively affected by the extent of unionization in the firm. It was also found that manufacturing firms invest significantly more in extensive search, by means of using more recruiting sources, than firms in agriculture, mining, construction, transportation or the services industries. Moreover, only firms in the transportation industry conduct significantly more interviews per hire than firms in the manufacturing sector, among firms in this sample. Characteristics of the labor market were not found to have any significant effects on employer extensive search.

*Intensive Search.* Intensity of search refers to the amount of information gathered about each individual in the applicant pool prior to making selection decisions. The intensity of employer search is captured in this study by the number of pre-employment selection tests the employer administers, as well as the extent of the employer's preference for informal over formal recruiting sources. Both of these measures of intensity of search are predicted to have a positive effect on the expected value of labor services, according to the theory presented in Chapter One. The operationalization of the factors hypothesized to have an effect on the employer's investment in intensive search were described in the preceding section of this chapter; the results of the estimations of the model are reported in Tables 3.8 and 3.9 and discussed in this section.

*Number of Selection Tests Administered.* There are a variety of selection tests available to employers for use in screening potential employees. In this study, the employer's decision whether to use five pre-employment selection tests was investigated. These selection tests included: ability tests, skills tests, drug tests, polygraphs,[11] and physical examinations. The factors that influence the use of these five selection tests, which represent intensive search, were analyzed and the results are reported in Table 3.8. The model accounts for thirty-one percent of the variance and has good overall fit (F = 13.429).

A number of firm-specific, labor-market and industry factors all influence a firm's choice of selection tests. As predicted, the extent of unionization and training available to workers, the percent of high-level workers, and firm size all positively and significantly affect the number of selection tests the employer will use, among firm-specific determinants. Although all the firm-specific determinants have coefficients greater than zero (*i.e.,* the predicted signs), UNION, TRAINING, PCTHIGH, and SIZE are the only four that are statistically significant.

Firms in the transportation industry are likely to use more selection tests for hiring than firms in manufacturing. Whereas, service industry firms are significantly likely to use *fewer* tests than manufacturing firms.

One characteristic of the labor market also significantly influences employer intensive search. Specifically, the intensity of employer search as measured by the use of selection tests increases significantly with the percentage of males in the firm's industry. The effect of both the percentage of whites and the level education in the firm's industry, while positive, were not found to be significant.

TABLE 3.8

*The Determinants of the Firm's Choice of Number of Selection Tests to Use*

| Explanatory Variable | Dependent Variable = TESTS | |
|---|---|---|
| | $\beta$ | Standard Deviation |
| Constant | -1.959 * | 1.168 |
| SIZE | 0.571E-05 *** | 0.245E-05 |
| UNION | 0.671 **** | 0.218 |
| PCTHIGH | -0.657 **** | 0.249 |
| VALUES | 0.674E-02 | 0.572E-02 |
| TRAINING | 0.755 **** | 0.125 |
| KEXP | 0.926E-01 | 0.135 |
| FIRE | -0.117 | 0.197 |
| AGMNCO | -0.296 | 0.197 |
| TRADE | -0.158 | 0.196 |
| TRANSPRT | 0.578 **** | 0.147 |
| SERVICE | -0.335 * | 0.175 |
| MGRADE | 0.622E-01 | 0.682E-01 |
| PCTMALE | 0.623E-02 * | 0.369E-02 |
| PCTWHITE | 0.166E-01 | 0.111E-01 |
| Adjusted-$R^2$ | .31 | |
| F-Statistic | 13.429 **** | |
| Sample Size | 380 | |

**** = $p < .01$; *** = $p < .025$; ** = $p < .05$; * = $p < .10$ (two-tailed tests); excluded industry is manufacturing.

*Percent of Informal Recruiting Sources Used.* As discussed in Chapter One, certain recruiting sources are likely to give an employer a competitive advantage in hiring because they offer the employer information concerning the expected value of the labor services of the job candidate that is not available to other prospective employers. Examples of such recruiting sources are employee referrals and internal candidates.[12] Because employers using these informal recruiting sources can make better estimates of the expected value of labor services of these individuals, *ceteris paribus*, they can improve the quality of their workforce by preferring the informal recruiting sources over formal ones.[13] The factors that lead an employer to prefer informal over formal recruiting sources and the direction of their hypothesized effects were outlined above; the results of the estimation of the model are found in Table 3.9.

Like the other measure of intensive search tested in this study (*i.e.,* the number of selection tests regularly administered to job candidates), the percent of informal recruiting sources used by the employer appears to be significantly influenced by some of all three types of specified factors.

Among the firm-specific factors that have a significant effect on the firm's preference for informal sources are the percent of both high-level and unionized workers in the firm. Both of these factors significantly reduce the firm's preference for informal over formal recruiting sources, as was predicted.[14]

With regard to industry differences, firms in both the wholesale and retail trade, and transportation industries are significantly more likely than firms in the manufacturing sector to prefer informal to formal recruiting sources.

And, among labor market factors, the level of education positively influences a firm's preference for informal recruiting sources as well, which supports the proposed hypothesis.

In sum, some factors in all three categories influence the employer's investment in intensive search as it was measured in this analysis. Firms in the transportation industry invest in intensive search both by using more tests and preferring informal recruiting sources, relative to manufacturing firms. Comparatively fewer pre-employment selection tests are used by firms in the services industry, in contrast. And firms in the trade industry are relatively more likely to prefer informal recruiting sources to those in manufacturing.

Intensive search is determined by both certain firm-specific and labor-market factors as well. In particular, larger firms, more unionized firms, firms with more high-level workers, and firms making formal training available to more employees use relatively more selection tests. The use of pre-employment selection tests is

TABLE 3.9

*The Determinants of the Percent of Informal Recruiting Sources Used*

| Explanatory Variable | Dependent Variable = PCTINFML | |
| --- | --- | --- |
| | $\beta$ | Standard Deviation |
| Constant | 0.302 * | 0.163 |
| SIZE | -0.428E-09 | 0.342E-08 |
| UNION | -0.531E-01 * | 0.304E-01 |
| PCTHIGH | -0.138 **** | 0.348E-01 |
| VALUES | 0.758E-03 | 0.800E-03 |
| TRAINING | 0.574E-02 | 0.175E-01 |
| KEXP | 0.128E-01 | 0.189E-01 |
| FIRE | -0.221E-01 | 0.276E-01 |
| AGMNCO | -0.175E-01 | 0.276E-01 |
| TRADE | 0.534E-01 * | 0.276E-01 |
| TRANSPRT | 0.465E-01 *** | 0.206E-01 |
| SERVICE | 0.836E-02 | 0.244E-01 |
| MGRADE | 0.200E-01 ** | 0.953E-02 |
| PCTMALE | -0.774E-04 | 0.516E-03 |
| PCTWHITE | -0.166E-02 | 0.156E-02 |
| Adjusted-$R^2$ | .05 | |
| F-Statistic | 2.368 **** | |
| Sample Size | 380 | |

**** = $p < .01$; *** = $p < .025$; ** = $p < .05$; * = $p < .10$ (two-tailed tests); excluded industry is manufacturing.

likewise positively affected by the percent male of workers in the firm's industry. Intensive search as captured by a preference for using Table 3.9 employee referrals and internal candidates over other recruiting sources is negatively influenced by the percent of both unionized workers and high level employees in the firm. These recruiting sources are also more likely to be preferred as the education level of workforce in the firm's industry rises.

## SECTION C: SUMMARY of RESULTS

The purpose of this chapter was to investigate the determinants of employers' recruitment and selection strategy investments. In particular, factors hypothesized to influence the following six specific hiring strategies were examined: the formal planning of recruitment and selection, the formal evaluation of the firm's recruitment and selection policies, the number of recruiting sources regularly used, the number of candidates to interview per hire, the number of selection tests to be used for screening candidates, and the firm's preference for informal versus formal recruiting sources. The first two hiring strategies are administrative practices that are measured on a firm-wide basis. The next two—the number of recruiting sources and the number of interviews per hire—are measures of employer extensive search. The last two recruitment and selection practices—the number of selection tests and the percent of recruiting sources used which are informal—are measures of employer intensive search. The factors hypothesized to affect these recruitment and selection strategies can be grouped as firm-specific, industry effects, and labor-market characteristics. The effects of these factors on a firm's choice of hiring strategies were tested using ordinary least squares regression (for measures of extensive and intensive search) and maximum likelihood estimation (for HR planning and evaluation). A summary of the findings is given in Table 3.10.

It was found that employers' investments in *extensive search* are predominantly influenced by certain firm-specific factors, especially the extent of unionization in the firm. The union effect was negative, as hypothesized. The number of interviews conducted per hire was found to be positively related to the firm's capital expenditures per employee. The number of recruiting sources used was positively influenced by both the extent of formal training programs and the percent of high-level workers in the firm.

Likewise, some industry effects were demonstrated in the test of the determinants of firms' extensive search as measured by both the number of recruiting sources used and the number of interviews conducted per hire. It was found that firms in transportation were significantly more likely both to use fewer recruiting sources to locate

TABLE 3.10

*Summary of the Results for the Determinants Model*

| | | | Extensive Search | | Intensive Search | |
|---|---|---|---|---|---|---|
| Explanatory Variables | HRPLAN | RSEVAL | INTRVS | SOURCES | TESTS | PCTINFML |
| SIZE | + | | | | + | |
| UNION | + | | - | - | + | - |
| PCTHIGH | | | | + | - | - |
| VALUES | + | | | | | |
| TRAINING | + | + | | + | + | |
| KEXP | | | + | | | |
| FIRE | | - | | | | |
| AGMNCO | | - | | - | | |
| TRADE | | | | | | + |
| TRANSPRT | - | - | + | - | + | + |
| SERVICE | | | | - | - | |
| MGRADE | | + | | | | + |
| PCTMALE | | | | | + | |
| Adjusted $R^2$ | .01 | .01 | .04 | .20 | .31 | .05 |

+/- = Significant at 10 percent level or better.

job applicants and to conduct more interviews per hire than firms in the manufacturing industry. Further, firms in agriculture, mining and construction, and the services industries also use significantly fewer recruiting sources than manufacturing firms.

With regard to the determinants of employer *intensive search*, it appears that certain characteristics of the labor market, in addition to some firm- and industry-specific factors have significant influence. The number of pre-employment selection tests was shown to rise with the percent male in the firm's industry. And an increase in the average education level of workers in the firm's industry causes firms to prefer informal recruiting sources to locate job candidates. Firms in the transportation industry are significantly more likely to use more tests for selection than firms in manufacturing; whereas service industry firms use significantly fewer. And firms in both the transportation and trade industries prefer informal recruiting sources relatively more than the comparison group as well.

Intensive search, as operationalized by the number of selection tests used, is more likely to occur in large firms, those that make formal training available to workers and have a relatively small percentage of high-level employees, and in heavily unionized firms. The preference for using informal recruiting sources was found to be negatively affected by the percent of both high-level employees and unionized workers in the firm.

Finally, a number of firm-specific factors predominate in firms' choice to engage in formal HR planning for staffing, whereas environmental factors appear to be more important in firms' decision to formally evaluate their staffing policies on a regular basis. In particular, firms in finance, insurance and real estate, agriculture, mining and construction, and the transportation industries are all significantly less likely than manufacturing firms to formally evaluate their staffing policies. In addition, the average level of education in the firm's industry increases the likelihood that firms will practice regular staffing function evaluation. While both HR planning and policy evaluation are positively influenced by the provision of training, more firm-specific characteristics including: the firm's size, the amount of employee participation, and the extent to which it is unionized, also positively influence its decision to practice formal HR planning.

The results of this analysis of the determinants of the firm's recruitment and selection strategies improve on the existing research in several ways. Within the HRM literature, there have been no studies to date of the determinants of a firm's choice of recruitment and selection strategies. This analysis contributes to the HRM literature by modeling and testing the determinants of the firm's hiring policies. Further, while labor economists have studied the determinants of recruitment and selection methods (*e.g.*, Holzer 1987, Bishop *et al.*, 1983), this analysis extends the literature by investigating the determinants of more recruitment and selection strategies than have been studied previously. Specifically, no previous labor economics studies have investigated the determinants of either human resource planning for staffing or the formal evaluation of hiring practices.

By offering a more precise picture of how firms differ in their recruitment and selection strategies as well as in how their businesses are organized and operated, this study makes an important contribution to improving our understanding of how the hiring process is determined. The more extensive our knowledge of the relationship of various firm-specific characteristics to the firm's choice of recruitment and selection strategies, the more clearly we can predict how hiring strategies will be altered as characteristics of the firm and environment change. Further, some of the characteristics included in this study are, in fact, currently changing, for instance, the provision of formal training is increasing in United States firms. From this analysis we know that as training increases, so does the firm's investment in search. Likewise, many firms are increasing employee involvement (see Delaney, Ichniowski, and Lewin 1989), which has also been shown to significantly increase employers' investments in some recruitment and selection strategies. Knowing which factors are significant determinants of a firm's hiring practices is likewise important because of the shrinking numbers of entry-level workers that firms have faced in the 1990s; competition for the best job candidates will increase and firms with the characteristics identified in this analysis will likely be able to hire the best job applicants because of their investments in intensive and extensive search.

These results also improve on previous research by virtue of better data than have been available for past analyses. Information from the Columbia HR Survey provided data on firm characteristics not previously available including, for example, the extent of formal training programs, and the employer's attitude towards employees. The survey also provided information regarding the recruitment and selection strategies used for workers in seven distinct occupational categories. Previous studies have only had information about the hiring strategy used for the last person hired.

Having investigated the determinants of firms' recruitment and selection strategies, and having shown that various firm-specific and environmental factors have significant effects on employers' investment in recruitment and selection strategies, I turn now to the effects of these investments on the productivity of the workforce.

## NOTES

1. The weights equal the percent of workers in each category.

2. Despite the fact that *direct applicants* (or walk-ins) is not a "formal" recruiting source *per se*, it is included in this category because it does not reveal any information that gives employers using it a comparative advantage in hiring over other employers, as do the use of employee referrals or internal candidates. See the theoretical model of Chapter One for a complete discussion of this.

3. Whether or not the organization provides formal training was asked in the Columbia HR survey for seven worker categories. The value of TRAINING equals the number of categories—zero to seven—to which the firm provides formal training, divided by the total number of categories in which the firm has workers. The worker categories are listed in Table 3.1 above (pg.42).

4. Of course, a better measure of the effects of capital expenditure on employer search strategies would be specific to the job or jobs being investigated. For example, expenditures for capital used by workers in each of the seven categories. However, these data are unavailable, so a firm-wide measure of capital expenditures is employed.

5. Including variables representing the characteristics of the labor market in the model controls for any systematic differences in the sample of job applicants each firm faces, and for variation in the search strategies of individuals in the labor market.

6. Jobs that require high-levels of education might require more intensive search. That is, the educational degree might be considered a sufficient certification of minimum qualification. Then interviews might be used to establish whether the individual "fits" with the organization. Unfortunately, the data used in the analysis do not allow me to test this.

7. See discussion on p.44 concerning the VALUES index, and the Appendix for how it was formulated.

8. The seven worker groups for which the question of formal training provision was posed include: managers, unionized and nonunionized professional and technical workers, unionized and nonunionized clerical workers, and unionized and nonunionized production and manufacturing employees.

9. It must be noted, however, that the actual value of this derivative varies from one firm to the next, and that the $\partial P/\partial X$ reported here represents the average for all firms in the sample. The derivative will be highest when the estimated probability of planning or evaluation is .5; it will be lower for any other probability estimates.

10. Recall that the variable SOURCES can take on values from zero to nine since there were data gathered on the use of nine different recruiting sources.

11. Data for this study were gathered prior to the passage of the Employee Polygraph Protection Act of 1988, which disallows the use of polygraphs tests for the selection of employees.

12. See the theoretical model section of Chapter One for a complete discussion (pp.20 and 21).

13. As noted above, the names "informal" and "formal" are slight misnomers because *direct applicants*, an informal recruiting source, are included in the latter category. See endnote 2 above.

14. Recall that the informal sources include both employee referrals and promotions-from-within. The presence of seniority clauses and testing provisions in collective bargaining contracts increase the use of internal promotions and therefore, would suggest that there be a positive coefficient on UNION in the PCTINFML equation. However, firms that are unionized may have reason to be predisposed to *avoid* using employee referrals as a recruiting source. Namely, these referrals may be relatively more sympathetic to unions than applicants from other recruiting sources, *ceteris paribus*. Thus,

this effect would suggest that there be a negative coefficient on UNION in the PCTINFML equation. In short, the effects of UNION on the use of employee referrals and of internal candidates respectively may be in conflict with one another. When PCTINFML was changed to include, first, only employee referrals, and second, only internal candidates, as recruiting sources, in the numerator, in fact, the results indicated that the effect of UNION was negative and significant ($\beta = -0.09$ with t-statistic = 3.531) and negative but not significant, respectively.

# CHAPTER FOUR

# The Labor Productivity Effects of Recruitment and Selection Strategies

It was shown in the last chapter that firms differ in their recruitment and selection strategies. Firms adopt recruitment and selection strategies and invest in them because they believe these organizational efforts will lead to a better quality workforce. In this chapter, I will explore the effects of variation in recruitment and selection strategies on the productivity of the firm's workforce.

Using the theoretical framework presented in Chapter One, it was hypothesized that increases in employer search at both the extensive and intensive margins, as well as the formal planning and evaluation of recruitment and selection strategies, lead to higher average labor productivity, *ceteris paribus*. The following specific hypotheses were derived from the theoretical framework.

It is expected that increasing extensive search by interviewing more candidates per hire and by using more recruiting sources will have a positive effect on labor productivity. Likewise, it is expected that increased intensive search, captured by the number of screening tests administered to each applicant, has a positive effect on labor productivity. Further, it has been hypothesized that preferring certain recruiting sources—namely, employee referrals and internal candidates—over formal recruiting sources will improve employer estimates of expected productivity, and therefore, result in better quality workers. Finally, it was hypothesized that engaging in HR planning for staffing, and the formal evaluation of staffing policies would both have positive effects on the productivity of the workforce.[1]

*71*

These hypotheses will be tested using the data described in Chapter Two. The next section of this chapter describes the empirical specification of the model. In the subsequent section, the results of the analysis are discussed.

## SECTION A: The EMPIRICAL MODEL

The productivity of a firm's workforce is determined by the interaction of the workers and the capital used in the production process. The manner in which workers and capital combine to produce output can be expressed by the Cobb-Douglas production function:

(1) $$Q = cL^{\beta_1}K^{\beta_2}\varepsilon$$

where L and K are measures of the labor of the workforce and capital respectively used to produce Q, the output; $\varepsilon$ is the error term and c is a constant.

Certain factors affect output (Q) through their effects on the labor variable (L), rather than having a direct effect on productivity. These factors influence the quality of the labor input. For example, the amount of formal training provided by the firm is expected to improve worker quality, and thereby increase the productivity of labor. Likewise, the variables of interest in this study, the firm's recruitment and selection procedures, affect productivity through their effects on the labor variable (L) in the manner outlined in the theoretical framework developed in Chapter One. The way in which these factors influence output levels via their interaction effects with labor can be expressed by expanding the labor variable (L) as follows:

(2) $$L = (1 + QL)^{\alpha}(AL)$$

where QL is a set of variables that affects the quality of the labor input. QL includes the firm's recruitment and selection strategy and other factors, and AL is the number of employees.

Similarly, other firm- or industry-specific characteristics affect the productivity of labor through their effects on capital expenditures of the firm. This relationship is given by the expression:

(3) $$K = (1 + FS)^{\theta}(AK)$$

where FS is a set of firm- or industry-specific factors that interacts with the firm's capital expenditures to affect the output levels and AK is the observed capital input.

In order to investigate the output per employee, or the labor productivity effects, equations (2) and (3) are substituted into equation (1) and both sides are divided by the number of employees (AL) to produce:

(4) $$Q/AL = c(1 + QL)^{\alpha\beta_1}AL^{\beta_1 - 1}(1 + FS)^{\theta\beta_2}(AK)^{\beta_2}\varepsilon$$

where Q/AL is the measure of labor productivity (LPROD) to be investigated.

A firm's organizational recruitment and selection efforts are among the factors hypothesized to influence labor productivity through their effects on labor quality. These factors are captured using measures of employer extensive and intensive search. Measures of extensive search are the number of interviews conducted per hire (IPERH), and the number of recruiting sources used regularly to generate applicants (SOURCES). Measures of intensive search include the number of selection tests regularly required of each job applicant and the firm's preference for informal over formal recruiting sources. TESTS and PREFINFM respectively are the names given to the variables representing these measures of intensive search. Other measures of a firm's recruitment and selection strategy include the formal planning of the hiring process (HRPLAN) and the formal and regular evaluation of recruitment and selection in the firm (RSEVAL). Both HRPLAN and RSEVAL are administrative policies that are hypothesized to improve the quality of the firm's recruitment and selection strategies, and therefore the quality of the resultant workforce.

Other factors likely to affect the quality of the workforce include the amount of formal training given to employees by the firm, and the extent of unionization of the workforce. These factors are included as controls in the equation to be estimated and they are called TRAIN and UNION respectively.[2]

The term QL, from equation (4), which contains variables affecting the quality of labor, can be expanded as follows:

(5)      $QL = (HRPLAN)^{\alpha_1}(RSEVAL)^{\alpha_2}(IPERH)^{\alpha_3}(SOURCES)^{\alpha_4}$
$(TESTS)^{\alpha_5}(PREFINFM)^{\alpha_6}(TRAIN)^{\alpha_7}(UNION)^{\alpha_8}$

Similarly, firms' capital expenditures can vary systematically with characteristics of the production process of the firm or industry. Further, the nature of the production process can change with the age of the product. For example, high technology firms are characterized by products at the early stages of their life cycle (Bartel and Lichtenberg 1987). These systematic differences are captured in the model by including a set of industry dummies as well as a measure to capture the age of the product, or its position in the product life cycle. The set of variables, FS, hypothesized to affect labor productivity through effects on the firm's capital expenditures, can be expressed:

(6)                      $FS = (INDUSTRY)^{\theta_1}(HITECH)^{\theta_2}$

Making substitutions and taking the logarithm of both sides, the following expression is obtained:[3]

(7)      $\ln(LPROD) = \ln(c) + \alpha_1\beta_1(HRPLAN) + \alpha_2\beta_1(RSEVAL) +$
$\alpha_3\beta_1(IPERH) + \alpha_4\beta_1(SOURCES) + \alpha_5\beta_1(TESTS) +$
$\alpha_6\beta_1(PREFINFM) + \alpha_7\beta_1(TRAIN) + \alpha_8\beta_1(UNION) +$
$(\beta_1-1)\ln(AL) + \theta_1\beta_2(INDUSTRY) +$
$\theta_2\beta_2(HITECH) + \beta_2\ln(K) + \ln(\varepsilon)$

It is assumed that the error term, $\ln(\varepsilon)$, is distributed randomly with a mean of zero and constant variance. After the log transformation, equation (7) can be estimated using ordinary least squares. The operationalization of the dependent and independent variable measures are specified in the next section. The results are discussed in the section that follows.

## SECTION B: The DEPENDENT and INDEPENDENT VARIABLES

*Dependent Variable.* The measure of the productivity of labor (LPROD) to be used in this analysis is given by the firm's net sales (in millions of dollars) per employee. Net sales per employee is a measure of firm performance per employee used in other studies (for example, see Clark 1984).[4] Data used to construct LPROD come from the 1986 Compustat II Industry Segment files (net sales) and from the Columbia HR Survey (employment figures) that was described in Chapter Two above.

*Independent Variables.* The independent variables of particular interest in this analysis are those that capture the recruitment and selection strategies of the firm. The data used to create the recruitment and selection strategies measures detailed here were gathered from the Columbia HR survey that was described in Chapter Two.

The first two recruitment and selection variables are measures of extensive search and are hypothesized to have a positive effect on labor productivity. The number of interviews per hire conducted by the firm is given by the variable IPERH. The value of IPERH is calculated as follows: the number of interviews per hire, for each of seven employee categories,[5] are weighted by the number of employees in each category respectively and summed across each firm's worker categories.[6] The second measure of extensive search is captured in the variable called SOURCES which equals the sum of the number of recruiting sources the firm regularly uses to hire workers in each of the seven worker categories, weighted by the number of employees in each category respectively and summed across the worker categories mentioned above (see endnote 5).

Two measures of intensive search are included in the empirical model: the first is the sum of the number of tests administered regularly to applicants for jobs in the seven worker categories as weighted by the number of employees in each category, and is called TESTS.[7] The second measure captures the degree to which the employer prefers informal to formal recruiting sources. Its value is equal to the percentage of the employer's regularly used recruiting sources that are informal (*i.e.,* either employee referrals or internal candidates). The variable in the analysis is called PREFINFM.[8] The coefficients on the variables IPERH, SOURCES, TESTS, and PREFINFM are expected to be greater than zero in the labor productivity equation.

The two administrative policies concerning recruitment and selection included in the model are the formal human resource planning of the staffing function, and the formal evaluation of the hiring function. The variables measuring whether or not firms practice these policies are called HRPLAN and RSEVAL respectively. The use of each of these practices is expected to have a positive impact on firm performance (Nkomo 1987, Scarpello and Ledvinka 1988, Craft 1980). They are coded as dichotomous variables that equal one if the firm practices them, and zero if not.

Table 4.1 gives a summary of the recruitment and selection methods used as explanatory variables, their variable names, and how they are operationalized.

*Control Variables.* Two other variables are contained in the term QL of equation (4) which represent factors that are hypothesized to affect the quality of the labor input to production. The first—the amount of formal training that the employer provides—is expected to improve workers' productivity levels. More importantly for this study, however, formal training can be used by the employer as a substitute for extensive and intensive recruitment and selection (Oi 1962), and therefore, it is included in the model as a control. Employer provision of training is measured in this analysis by a variable called TRAINING. The value of this variable equals the percent of employee categories in which the firm offers formal training programs (see endnote 5 above for specific categories). The sign of the coefficient on TRAINING is expected to be positive. Training data were obtained from the Columbia HR survey.

The second factor from the term QL to be entered into the model which is also likely to affect labor productivity is the extent of unionization of the workforce. Freeman and Medoff (1984) report that "most studies of productivity find that unionized establishments are more productive than otherwise comparable nonunion establishments" (p.169). The effect of unionization is controlled for in this analysis by the inclusion of a variable called UNION. UNION equals the percentage of the firm's workforce that is covered by collective bargaining (as reported by the employer in the Columbia HR survey) and it is expected that the coefficient on this variable will be greater than zero.

The variable used in the analysis to represent average labor input (AL) is given by the number of employees in the firm. The number of employees, or firm size, is expected to have a positive effect on productivity, *ceteris paribus*, because larger firms are likely to benefit from greater economies of scale than smaller firms. Data for this variable were obtained from the Columbia HR survey.

Recall that the dependent variable is given by net sales *per employee*; to use the number of employees to represent the firm's average labor input means that I am including the same measure (in part) on both sides of the equation. Hence, the elasticity of net sales with respect to the labor input is estimated by adding one to the coefficient on AL.

TABLE 4.1

*Recruitment and Selection Methods Used as Independent Variables in the Performance Model*

| Variable Name | Definition |
|---|---|
| **Extensive Search** | |
| IPERH | Weighted sum of number of interviews conducted per hire.[a] |
| SOURCES | Weighted sum of number of recruiting sources regularly used to generate applicants.[a] |
| **Intensive Search** | |
| TESTS | Weighted sum of number of selection tests regularly administered to applicants.[a,b] |
| PREFINFM | Weighted sum of percentage of firm's recruiting sources that are informal.[a,c] |
| **Administrative Policies** | |
| HRPLAN | Equals one if firm engages in formal HR Planning for Staffing and Selection. |
| RSEVAL | Equals one if firm engages in formal Evaluation of Staffing and Selection Policy. |

[a] Sums include seven worker categories: managers, unionized and nonunionized professional and technical workers, unionized and nonunionized clerical workers, and unionized and nonunionized manufacturing and production workers, and are weighted by the number of workers in each category.
[b] Selection tests include: ability tests, skill tests, polygraphs, drug tests and physical examinations.
[c] Informal recruiting sources include: employee referrals and in-house candidates; formal recruiting sources include: newspaper advertisements, undergraduate institutions, graduate and professional institutions, direct applicants, private and public employment agencies, and search firms.

The variable used to represent the firm's investment in capital (*i.e.,* K in equation (7) ) is given by a measure of its total assets and is called CAPITAL. CAPITAL is equal to the firm's identifiable assets in millions of dollars. CAPITAL is expected to have a coefficient greater than zero ($\beta_2 > 0$) because the marginal value product of labor rises with capital stock. Data for CAPITAL come from the 1986 Compustat II Industry Segment files and the Columbia HR survey.

TABLE 4.2

*Dependent and Control Variables in the Performance Model*

| Variable Name | Definition |
| --- | --- |
| LPROD | Net Sales (in millions of dollars) divided by the number of employees. |
| ALABOR | Total number of employees in firm. |
| TRAINING | Percent of worker categories offered formal training programs.[a] |
| UNION | Percent of firm's employees covered by collective bargaining. |
| HITECH | Equals one if firm is in high-technology category. |
| CAPITAL | Amount of firm's assets in millions of dollars. |
| AGMNCO | Equals one if firm is in agriculture, mining or construction industry. |
| FIRE | Equals one if firm is in finance, insurance or real estate industry. |
| MANU[b] | Equals one if firm is in manufacturing industry. |
| TRAN | Equals one if firm is in transportation industry. |
| TRADE | Equals one if firm is in wholesale or retail trade industry. |
| SERV | Equals one if firm is in service industry. |

[a] The seven worker categories include: managers, unionized and nonunionized professional and technical workers, unionized and nonunionized clerical workers, and unionized and nonunionized manufacturing and production workers.
[b] This is the excluded industrial group in the regression analysis.

The age of the firm's product is represented by a dummy variable called HITECH; HITECH equals one if the firm is a high technology firm and zero otherwise.[9] The coefficient on HITECH is expected to be positive because high technology products are at the early stages of their life cycle, where the rate of output is rapidly increasing (Bartel and Lichtenberg 1987).

Finally, groupings of 2-digit SIC industry dummies are included in the model in order to capture the effects of other unobservable structural differences that may affect investment in capital stock differentially across industries. Moreover, industry dummies are included to control for any systematic differences in wage offers and hiring standards across industries. Five dummy variables are included in the equation to represent the following industrial groups: (1) finance, insurance and real estate (FIRE), (2) agriculture, mining and construction (AGMNCO), (3) wholesale and retail trade (TRADE), (4) transportation (TRAN), and (5) service industries (SERV). The excluded industrial group represents firms in (6) manufacturing. No predictions are made as to how these variables are expected to affect labor productivity *a priori*.

Table 4.2 presents a list of the variables in the performance model and how each is defined. We turn now to the results of the empirical analysis.

# SECTION C: RESULTS of the EMPIRICAL ANALYSIS

The means and standard deviations of the variables used in the OLS analysis are presented in Table 4.3. As pointed out in Chapter Two, each observation in the analysis is a business line, rather than an entire firm. There are a total of 495 business lines in the sample.

The labor productivity measure used—net sales per employee (LPROD)—has an average value of $544,919 in 1986 sales per employee. The range of LPROD was from a minimum of $311 to a maximum of $33.5 million.

The majority of business units in the sample formally evaluate their staffing policies (86 percent) while only 42 percent have formal, written plans for recruitment and selection. On average, five interviews are conducted for each employee hired.[10] With a maximum possible value of nine (*i.e.*, nine possible recruiting sources), the average number of regularly used recruiting sources used by a firm is over four. Likewise, with a maximum possible of five (*i.e.*, five selection tests), the average firm administers approximately one pre-employment selection test on a regular basis to applicants of all levels. Finally, forty percent of the recruiting sources regularly used by the average firm in the sample are informal, which includes employee referrals and internal candidates.

Results of the regression analyses are reported in Table 4.4. The model explained eighty-one percent of the variance (adjusted $R^2$ = .81) and eight of the sixteen variables are significant at the ten percent level or better.

TABLE 4.3

*Mean Values of Variables in Performance Model (Standard Deviation = SD)*

| Variable | Mean | SD |
|---|---|---|
| Measure of Performance | | |
| Labor Productivity (LPROD) | 0.545 | 2.353 |
| (Net sales per employee in $ millions) | | |
| | | |
| Recruitment and Selection Methods | | |
| HR Planning (HRPLAN) | 0.419 | 0.494 |
| R&S Evaluation (RSEVAL) | 0.857 | 0.351 |
| Interviews/Hire (IPERH) | 5.224 | 4.408 |
| Recruiting Sources (SOURCES) | 4.442 | 1.445 |
| Number of Selection Tests (TESTS) | 1.180 | 1.067 |
| Percent Informal Sources (PREFINFM) | 0.396 | 0.130 |
| | | |
| Control Variables | | |
| Firm Size (ALABOR) | 6082.142 | 18853.166 |
| Percent Unionized (UNION) | 0.181 | 0.266 |
| Percent of occupations with formal | | |
| training programs (TRAIN) | 0.403 | 0.414 |
| Capital stock in $ millions (CAPITAL) | 1582.393 | 6631.605 |
| High-Technology (HITECH) | 0.099 | 0.299 |
| Industry: | | |
| Agric., Mining, Constr. (AGMNCO) | 0.065 | 0.246 |
| Fin., Insur., R. Estate (FIRE) | 0.119 | 0.324 |
| Manufacturing (MANU) | 0.465 | 0.499 |
| Wholesale, retail trade (TRADE) | 0.075 | 0.263 |
| Transportation (TRAN) | 0.162 | 0.368 |
| Service (SERV) | 0.115 | 0.320 |

NB: Number of firms used to calculate means ranges from 410 to 495 due to missing data.

Two of the recruitment and selection variables have the predicted signs (*i.e.,* they are both positive), but the four others do not.[11] The hypotheses regarding extensive and intensive search both received partial support. Extensive search, as measured by the number of recruiting sources the employer regularly uses has a positive and significant effect on labor productivity. Moreover, intensive search, as measured by the number of selection tests used, also positively and significantly improves labor productivity.

Labor productivity rises significantly with the number of selection tests the firm administers to prospective employees. In other words, there are real gains to the employer who searches more intensively for information about the expected value of labor services among individuals in the available labor market. This effect is shown to be the largest and most statistically significant of all the recruitment and selection strategies in its effect on worker performance.

In addition, for each additional recruiting source the employer uses on a regular basis, there is a significant increase in net sales per employee; this effect is significant at the ten percent level. Thus, there are significant gains to searching for employees more broadly, or, by tapping more recruiting sources.

The results for the other recruitment and selection variables are contrary to expected findings; however, the negative labor productivity effects are not significantly different from zero.

The results for the control variables are as expected, with two exceptions. The labor elasticity is estimated to be about 0.2 and is significant at the less than one percent level (t-statistic = 32.570). The firm's capital stock also has a positive and highly significant effect on net sales per employee, as expected. However, the amount of training provided for employees was found to have a negative, albeit not significant effect on labor productivity. Further, labor productivity was shown to vary positively (but not significantly) with the extent of unionism, as predicted.

Four of the five industry dummies have negative and significant effects on net sales per employee: agriculture, mining and construction, transportation, finance, insurance and real estate and services industries.[12] The effects of the trade industries are positive, as compared with the excluded industry of manufacturing, and statistically significant. Finally, although the effect of product age as

TABLE 4.4

*The Effects of Recruitment and Selection Strategies on Labor Productivity
(standard deviation = SD)*

| Explanatory Variable | Dependent Variable = LPROD (log) | |
| --- | --- | --- |
| | $\beta$ | SD |
| Constant | -0.115 | 0.239 |
| HRPLAN | -0.210E-01 | 0.755E-01 |
| RSEVAL | -0.871E-01 | 0.108 |
| IPERH | -0.852E-02 | 0.740E-02 |
| SOURCES | 0.496E-01 * | 0.291E-01 |
| TESTS | 0.937E-01 *** | 0.398E-01 |
| PREFINFM | -0.216 | 0.304 |
| ALABOR (log) | -0.845 **** | 0.259E-01 |
| TRAINING | -0.587E-01 | 0.935E-01 |
| UNION | 0.215 | 0.169 |
| CAPITAL (log) | 0.823 **** | 0.238E-01 |
| FIRE | -1.258 **** | 0.130 |
| AGMNCO | -0.702 **** | 0.165 |
| TRANSPORTATION | -0.632 **** | 0.112 |
| TRADE | 0.641 **** | 0.151 |
| SERVICE | -0.138 | 0.122 |
| HITECH | -0.147 | 0.124 |
| Adjusted $R^2$: | .81 | |
| F Statistic: | 92.659 **** | |
| Sample Size: | 334 | |

**** = $p < .01$; *** = $p < .025$; ** = $p < .05$; * = $p < .10$; excluded industrial group is manufacturing.

captured by HITECH is negative, the result is not statistically significant.

Table 4.5 reports the regression results for the model with two of the variables reformulated. Specifically, the variable TESTS is separated into SKILL TESTS and OTHER TESTS (which includes physical examinations, polygraphs, drug and aptitude tests), and PREFINFM is disaggregated into INTERNAL PROMOTIONS and EMPLOYEE REFERRALS. INTERNAL PROMOTIONS is measured by the weighted percentage of nonentry-level jobs that have been filled from internal sources in recent years. EMPLOYEE REFERRALS is given by a weighted average of the number of job categories for which employee referrals are used as a regular recruiting source.

Disaggregating TESTS into SKILL and OTHER TESTS is done in order to investigate whether screening for job skills has a greater effect on labor productivity than the types of things screened for in the other tests. It was thought that if an individual possesses the requisite skills to perform the job, then labor productivity should be relatively more improved than if the individual was found to have an aptitude for the work, not display signs of drug usage, to be honest or to be in good physical shape (*i.e.*, qualities for which the other selection tests screened). In short, screening for skills should be the relatively most important factor when measuring labor productivity effects among the dimensions being screened; therefore the effect of SKILL TESTS should be greater than of OTHER TESTS on labor productivity.

Using INTERNAL PROMOTIONS and EMPLOYEE REFERRALS, in lieu of PREFINFM, is done to see if the use of these recruiting sources has a direct effect on labor productivity. The fact that certain recruiting sources are used almost exclusively for certain types of workers (*e.g.*, search firms are used primarily to recruit managers) could be confounding the hypothesized effects of internal promotions and employee referrals on labor productivity when using PREFINFM to test the hypothesis. It was speculated that this could be the reason that PREFINFM was negative and insignificant in the analysis whose results are reported in Table 4.4. By separating the variable into two, we can observe the independent effects of the use of these two recruiting sources on labor productivity. It is expected that the effects of all four variables (*i.e.*, SKILL TESTS, OTHER TESTS, INTERNAL PROMOTIONS, and EMPLOYEE REFERRALS) will be greater than zero.

TABLE 4.5

*The Effects of Recruitment and Selection Strategies on Labor Productivity*
*(standard deviation = SD)*

| Explanatory Variable | Dependent Variable = LPROD (log) | |
| | $\beta$ | SD |
| --- | --- | --- |
| Constant | -0.413 | 0.203 |
| HRPLAN | -0.125E-01 | 0.768E-01 |
| RSEVAL | -0.594E-01 | 0.113 |
| IPERH | -0.922E-02 | 0.745E-02 |
| SOURCES | 0.659E-01 * | 0.348E-01 |
| SKILL TESTS | 0.277 *** | 0.115 |
| OTHER TESTS | 0.342E-01 | 0.487E-01 |
| INTERNAL PROMOTIONS | 0.270E-02 ** | 0.134E-02 |
| EMPLOYEE REFERRALS | -0.487E-02 | 0.165 |
| ALABOR (log) | -0.849 **** | 0.260E-01 |
| TRAINING | -0.115 | 0.974E-01 |
| UNION | 0.222 | 0.178 |
| CAPITAL (log) | 0.824 **** | 0.241E-01 |
| FIRE | -1.356 **** | 0.138 |
| AGMNCO | -0.671 **** | 0.171 |
| TRANSPORTATION | -0.653 **** | 0.114 |
| TRADE | 0.633 **** | 0.152 |
| SERVICE | -0.189 | 0.125 |
| HITECH | -0.145 | 0.125 |

| | |
| --- | --- |
| Adjusted $R^2$: | .82 |
| F Statistic: | 83.920 **** |
| Sample Size: | 318 |

**** = $p < .01$; *** = $p < .025$; ** = $p < .05$; * = $p < .10$; excluded industrial group is manufacturing.

The results in Table 4.5 support the hypotheses. Indeed, using skill tests as a selection instrument has a strong positive effect on labor productivity. While the effect of the other selection tests is still positive, it is not statistically significant (t = 0.702). It is also the case that the independent effect of the use of promotions-from-within on labor productivity is positive. However, contrary to expectations, the effect of employee referrals is negative, albeit statistically insignificant.

The signs on the other variables remain the same. We still observe positive and significant effects of the number of regularly used recruiting sources on labor productivity, while the other three recruitment and selection variables show no statistically significant influence. In addition, the direction and magnitude of the control variables are virtually identical to the results reported in Table 4.4.

## NOTES

1. It should be noted that over time, causality may be hard to establish. More precisely, in the long run, greater productivity may stimulate greater search investments, as opposed to the reverse order. However, following Holzer (1987), in the short run (*i.e.,* at any given point in time), institutional investments in various search strategies are assumed to be fixed.

2. As discussed in Chapter One, the availability of training can reasonably be taken to be exogenous to recruiting and selection decisions in the short run because the provision of training to employees is a longer run decision "embodied in contracts or bureaucratic practices that are not easily changed" (Holzer 1987 p.253).

3. The equation (7) transformation uses the approximation $ln(1 + x) =\_\sim x$ for small $x$.

4. While some measure of value added per employee would have been a desirable measure of productivity, this information is not available by business unit.

5. The seven worker categories include: managers, unionized professional and technical workers, nonunionized professional and technical workers, unionized clericals, nonunionized clericals, unionized production and manufacturing workers, and nonunionized production and manufacturing workers.

6. Ideally, IPERH should be weighted by the number of hires per worker category, not the number of employees per worker category. However, this information was not available.

7. Firms in the sample provided information about their regular use of the following selection tests: aptitude tests, skill tests, polygraphs, drug tests and physical examinations.

8. The informal recruiting sources include employee referrals and internal candidates. The formal recruiting sources include newspaper advertisements, undergraduate and graduate institutions, private and government employment agencies, walk-ins and search firms.

9. Firms are classified as high-technology firms by means of the classification system employed by Bartel and Lichtenberg (1987 p.168), which is based on firm expenditures on research and development.

10. The range on this variable is from a low of less than one interview per hire to a high of fifty-one interviews per hire. Note that the number of interviews was weighted by the percentage of the firm's workers in the category.

11. Although not statistically significant, the coefficients for the other recruitment and selection variables are as follows: HRPLAN ($\beta$ = -.0210, with t-statistic = 0.279), RSEVAL ($\beta$ = -.0871, with t-statistic = 0.806), IPERH ($\beta$ = -.0085, with t-statistic = 1.151), and PERFINFM ($\beta$ = -.2164, with t-statistic = 0.712).

12. The one exception is that the service industry effect, while negative, was not statistically significant.

# CHAPTER FIVE

# Summary and Conclusions

This volume has addressed the following two questions: (a) what factors influence employers' use of certain recruitment and selection strategies? and (b) what effects do these recruitment and selection strategies have on employee performance? The analyses were conducted in an effort to extend the research concerning the recruitment and selection processes from the employer's perspective.

The specific recruitment and selection strategies studied in this book included employer extensive search (as measured by both the number of interviews conducted per hire, and the number of recruiting sources regularly used), employer intensive search (as measured by the number of pre-employment selection tests administered to job candidates, and the percent of the employer's chosen recruiting sources that are informal), and two administrative policies—human resources planning for recruitment and selection, and the formal evaluation of hiring policies.

In this chapter, I will discuss the contributions this study makes to the literature, the conclusions to be drawn from and the implications of what was learned, and the strengths and weaknesses of the framework and data used to perform the analyses in this volume.

## SECTION A: FINDINGS

*Regarding Human Resource Planning for Recruitment and Selection and the Evaluation of Hiring Policies.* The existing literature did not give guidance as to what types of firms are likely to engage in human resource planning (HR planning) for recruitment and selection (see Delaney, Ichniowski and Lewin 1988, for a study of the determinants of general HR planning). Thus, one contribution of this study was to specify certain firm-specific and environmental factors predicted to influence firms to engage in HR planning for hiring. It was found that HR planning depends upon firm-specific characteristics for the most part. In particular, it was demonstrated that firms that are large, that highly value their employees, that provide formal training to employees, and that are highly unionized, are relatively more likely to engage in HR planning.

It has been hypothesized in the literature (Walker 1980, Craft 1980) that engaging in HR planning will improve firm performance; the specific mechanism by which this outcome is achieved is through "help(ing) managers anticipate and meet changing needs relating to the acquisition, deployment, and utilization of people" (Walker 1980 p.10). It was hypothesized in this study that firms that engage in the formal planning of recruitment and selection strategies would demonstrate greater labor productivity, *ceteris paribus*. The predicted effect of HR planning on employee performance (as measured by net sales per employee) was less than zero, but not statistically significant. As has been suggested (Delaney, Ichniowski and Lewin 1988), perhaps the variable used to measure HR planning for recruitment and selection was not sufficient by itself to capture a complex relationship. That is, reporting that HR planning for recruitment and selection is undertaken in the business unit is not a detailed enough measure to identify those business units that are able to benefit significantly from this hiring activity. A business unit indicating that it engages in HR planning for recruitment and selection could, on the one hand, practice sophisticated forecasting techniques for HR needs and conduct needs analyses using extensive and detailed HRIS data bases; on the other hand, the same answer could mean merely that several people talk informally about how many people should be hired.

The effect of the formal evaluation of recruitment and selection policies on labor performance was not found to be significantly different from zero either. However, an interesting difference between the determinants of the formal evaluation of recruitment and selection policies and HR planning was found; namely, the firm's choice to formally evaluate its hiring policies is significantly driven, in part, by a response to environmental factors and much less in response to organizational characteristics. This is the opposite of the case for HR planning, where firm-specific characteristics were found to be relatively more important than environmental factors as determinants. Specifically, there are significant industrial differences: firms in finance, real estate, and insurance, agriculture, mining and construction, as well as those in the transportation industry are all less likely than manufacturing firms to practice the formal and regular evaluation of hiring policies. Furthermore, the educational level of workers in the firm's industry is positively associated with the evaluative function.

These findings suggest that certain firms, regardless of their industry or labor market conditions, are likely to choose to do HR planning, whereas, certain environmental characteristics are more important in their decision to engage in the formal evaluation of recruitment and selection strategies. The decision to engage in HR planning—a function that is the more proactive of the two—appears to depend primarily upon the people in the organization and how much they allow their employees to participate in management decisions, as opposed to what is going on in the environment. Nonetheless, neither administrative HR function was shown to significantly enhance labor productivity.

*Regarding Employer Extensive Search.* Extensive search by employers for information concerning job applicants was measured in this study by the number of interviews conducted per hire and the number of regularly used recruiting sources.

The extant literature does not address the question of what factors determine the number of interviews per hire that the firm will conduct. In a closely-related study (Bishop *et al.,* 1983), however, it was found that certain firm-specific characteristics positively influence the number of interviews per offer conducted by the firm—among them, the firm size, training, clerical positions, and having advance notice of the job opening. The percentage unionized was found to be a negative determinant of the number of interviews per offer. The results of my work support these findings, and add that capital expenditures also positively influence the number of interviews per hire. To my knowledge, no previous study has examined the number of recruiting sources regularly used to locate potential workers.

In this study, it was found that we know more about which factors determine the number of recruiting sources to be used regularly to generate job candidates, than we do about the factors determining how many candidates will be interviewed per hire. Both measures of extensive search are negatively affected by an increasingly unionized workforce. It was hypothesized that certain procedures governing hiring methods that are negotiated in collective bargaining agreements are the reason for this result. That is, there may be negotiated rules for the manner in which jobs are to be filled (*e.g.*, by seniority or by test scores), which reduce the number of needed interviews and the number and types of recruiting sources to be used to find potential workers. The number of worker groups given formal training, and the percent of high level workers both are positively associated with the number of recruiting sources used.

Increasing the number of interviews administered per hire was not shown to significantly improve employee performance, for business units in this sample.

However, it was shown that increases in the number of recruiting sources used to locate job applicants has a positive effect on the performance of workers. In other words, increasing the avenues by which an applicant pool is amassed pays off in labor productivity gains. This means that employers would benefit from exploring new ways of and places for locating prospective employees. From the results of this study, it has been demonstrated that increases in different recruiting sources to find new employees will benefit the employer with a more productive workforce.

*Regarding Employer Intensive Search.* Intensive search by employers for information concerning job applicants was measured by both the number of screening devices used in selection, and favoring the use of internal promotions and employee referrals as recruiting sources over other recruiting sources.

We know from the extant literature that certain selection tests are used primarily for some types of workers; for instance, manual skill tests are likely to be employed in the selection of secretaries and manual workers, while physical exams are usually required of potential managers. The literature, however, does not guide us about how many selection tests are used to hire workers, nor which factors lead firms to prefer the use of employee referrals and promotions-from-within over other sources for job candidates. Holzer's work (1987) showed that for the last employee hired, employee referrals were "used less frequently by larger firms and in recruiting to fill jobs that require a college education" (p.261), but his work does not address the determinants of the comparative use of employee referrals to other recruiting sources.

In this analysis, it was found that both measures of intensive search were negatively affected by the percent of high level workers in the business unit. The percent unionized increased the number of selection tests used, but significantly decreased the preference for recruiting from employee referrals or internal candidates. Larger business units, those that provide formal worker training, and those that operate in industries with a high percentage of male workers are all relatively likely to require more selection tests of job applicants, *ceteris paribus*.

Increasing the number of pre-employment selection tests was shown to significantly improve the productivity of labor. In other words, collecting more information about each job candidate prior to making hiring decisions will enhance the quality of the employment match made. Anecdotal evidence from Japanese corporations has suggested that this is true. In Japanese firms, there are great investments in the amount of information gathered about each applicant prior to hiring some. Moreover, it was found that screening for job skills has the greatest effect on labor productivity among the selection instruments analyzed. The use of other screening tests positively, but not significantly, affects labor productivity when disaggregated.

We know from extant literature and empirical studies about the effects of certain recruiting sources on employee performance both for employees within one organization (Taylor and Schmidt 1983, Breaugh and Mann 1984, Hill 1970, Caldwell and Spivey 1983, and Decker and Cornelius 1979), and for the last employee hired across organizations (Holzer 1987). This study attempted to show that employee performance is improved by recruiting workers internally or through employee referrals in lieu of using other recruiting sources; while the relationship was positive, it was not, however, statistically significant. Nevertheless, when the variable was reconfigured to capture the independent effects of the use of internal promotions and employee referrals on labor productivity it was shown that using promotions-form-within has a significantly positive influence. The effect of employee referrals was not significant, however.

## SECTION B: CONCLUSIONS and IMPLICATIONS

One conclusion that can be drawn from this study is that firms differ significantly in their recruitment and selection strategies. In particular, it was found that firm characteristics especially matter in determining how an organization will recruit and select its workforce. While some firm-specific factors are more consistent in their effects than others, and some do not appear to have significant effects at all, an important finding of this investigation is that characteristics of the firm significantly and consistently influence its chosen recruitment and selection investment strategy.

Another important finding of this study is that although HR planning for recruitment and selection and the formal evaluation of hiring policies did not appear to have significant effects on the productivity of the employees, investments in both extensive and intensive search by employers do. Recruitment and selection strategies demonstrated to have a significantly positive effect on employee performance include: using more recruiting sources to generate job applicants, using more selection tests, particularly skill tests, to screen potential job holders, and using internal promotions as a source to fill jobs.

A number of implications of importance to employers can be derived from these results. The first is that in order to improve employee performance, more care must be taken in procuring a workforce. Even before any training, development or reward systems can improve the performance of an organization's workers, efforts put into maximizing the quality of the employment match will pay off in higher levels of productivity. That is to say, employers should not depend upon being able to "mold" employees once they are in the firm, but rather, they should take the time and make the necessary investments to find the right workers in the market.

Second, employers would do well to scan the labor market extensively. They should search for job applicants via new and multiple recruiting sources. Scanning the labor market is especially important in light of the changes in the characteristics of today's workforce. To begin with, firms are currently facing a shortage of entry-level workers. And the number of young workers continues to shrink into the mid-1990s; the "baby bust" generation, or Generation X,—or those people born from approximately 1962 to 1975—is joining the labor force now and their numbers are causing fierce competition for entry-level workers among employers. Further, the average age of workers is rising; by 2000, the average American worker will be approximately fifty years old. In addition, the number of women in the labor force has been steadily increasing. A question for employers is how to locate and hire the best among these new types of workers. The changing profile of the American worker, in addition to the results of this study suggest that the use of new recruiting sources should be beneficial to employers. For instance, the increase in racial and ethnic diversity among American workers suggests tapping job candidates through non-English newspapers and other ethnic publications; likewise, the aging of the United States' workforce suggests employers look for new employees through senior organizations or other groups to which elderly people seeking employment may belong.

A third implication of this study is that organizations should use more screening devices when selecting workers in order to collect more information about each applicant in the pool. Skill, aptitude, drug, polygraph tests and physical examinations were included in the present study. And the use of more of them per applicant, among business units in this sample, resulted in improved employment matches as demonstrated by significantly higher worker productivity, *ceteris paribus*. Further, the use of skill tests in particular has been shown to significantly improve the performance of employees. Thus, one of the most important dimensions to screen for when hiring is the presence of job skills.

The productivity benefits of increasing all types of selection testing may be thwarted in the United States by recent trends that would limit the use of some tests by employers. For example, the use of polygraph tests for employment decision purposes was recently outlawed by the Congress. Likewise, there have been lawsuits brought and arguments made against employers' right to use drug testing for employment decisions. Drug and genetic testing are viewed by many as an invasion of the applicant's privacy and should, for that reason, be disallowed. Indeed, some states have banned the use of genetic screening for employment purposes. Therefore, it may be the case that in spite of the gains to labor productivity demonstrated in this study, employers' rights to increase their use of certain types of selection testing may be limited in the future. Given that skill tests were shown to have the greatest effect on productivity, limitations on other types of testing might not be so important to employers.

A fourth implication of this study is that employers are encouraged to use promotions-from-within to fill nonentry level vacancies within the organization. Internal promotions enhance employee performance. This makes a certain amount of common sense: people hired from within know the organization better than those hired externally, their longer average tenure enhances the likelihood that they will remain with the employer, and the prospects of advancement within the organization will serve as a motivator for all employees. The use of internal promotions to fill vacancies also points to the great importance of taking care in hiring for entry-level positions. Employers would do well to invest in search strategies for entry-level positions, especially at the managerial level, if they engage in internal promotion as a regular policy.

Finally, it was found here that the business units which are more likely to engage in the recruitment and selection strategies that have been shown to positively affect labor productivity are larger, less unionized, and provide formal training to their workers. Business units in the transportation industry are also more likely to invest in these strategies. This result has implications for individuals in their job searches. That is, when seeking new jobs, individuals will be attracted to organizations that invest in the recruitment and selection strategies that lead to better employment matches, in order to maximize their own fit with the job. Thus, the best candidates should be attracted to large, nonunion organizations that have formal training programs available for their workforces.

It should be noted that, due to the nature of the sample used in this research, the conclusions and implications presented here may be more applicable to larger firms than smaller ones.

## SECTION C: STRENGTHS and WEAKNESSES of the STUDY

In this book, I have attempted to increase our understanding of the determinants and effects of various recruitment and selection strategies used by a sample of 495 business units today.

The performance-effects model was shown to be relatively valid; that is, from it, we know a fair amount about which factors affect labor productivity for business units in this sample (*i.e.*, $R^2 =$ .81). The unexplained variance may be in part do to imperfect measures for some of the variables, including those measuring HR planning for recruitment and selection, and the formal evaluation of hiring policies. As stated above, all of these variables could be more complex than the measures that were employed allowed for.

With regard to the determinants of recruitment and selection strategies, much of the variance was not accounted for by the model. The model performs best for the number of selection tests administered per applicant (*i.e.*, $R^2 = .31$) and the number of recruiting sources used (*i.e.*, $R^2 = .20$). Clearly, from the results of this investigation, we have not learned much about what factors determine HR planning for hiring, the evaluation of hiring policies, the number of interviews per hire, and the business unit's preference for certain informal over formal recruiting sources.

Several improvements to the study and further questions for investigation have been suggested by this work. First, this analysis would be enhanced by the refinement of some of the variables— specifically, more detailed measures of some of the recruitment and selection strategies, especially the administrative policies, and the inclusion of some geographically specific measures of labor force characteristics. An effort to locate measures of the omitted variables in the determinants model would improve the work done here. In the future, for example, further tests of the kind conducted here could be carried out on a smaller scale that would allow for the collection of more accurate measures of these variables.

Another possible weakness of this study, as was mentioned above (Chapter Four, endnote 1), is that the model used is not a simultaneous model. That is, in the longer run, greater productivity may stimulate greater investments in employer-search strategies. This is a question that could be addressed in further studies. However, in this study, I estimated a recursive model, and did not look at the effects of labor productivity on employers' search strategy investment decisions.

Understanding why firms use the recruitment and selection procedures that they do, and the effects that their chosen hiring methods have on employee performance are important research questions for two very practical reasons. Recruitment and selection both cost a lot and these functions determine the composition of the organization's labor force. Employers need to know which recruitment and selection strategies will result in the most productive work force for them. From this study, we know that increasing extensive and intensive search will obtain this desired result.

# Appendix

## DETAILS CONCERNING the DATA BASE

The database used for this dissertation came from a larger one that was gathered under the aegis of John Delaney, Casey Ichniowski and David Lewin of the Industrial Relations Research Center at the Columbia University Graduate School of Business in 1986-1987.

The unit of analysis in the database is the *business unit*, as opposed to the entire firm. A business unit is defined as any portion of a corporation responsible for generating ten percent or more of sales and assets. Reporting corporate information by business unit, as opposed to firm-wide level, was recommended by the Financial Accounting Standards Board (FASB) in Statement of Financial Accounting Standards Number 14 (SFAS No.14). Information for separate business units is reported in both corporate annual reports and in 10-K reports which are filed with the Securities and Exchange Commission. In light of the wide diversification among United States corporations at the time of this study, financial and economic information reported by business unit, rather than by company, gives a clearer picture of the level of economic activity within industries.

Standard and Poor's Compustat II database contains economic and financial information for business units of United States firms. Using the name and address file maintained by the Standard and Poor's Compustat Services, a list of 7,765 executives in charge of these business units in United States, publicly held corporations was compiled. A questionnaire about Human Resources policies, developed by Delaney, Ichniowski and Lewin, was distributed in 1986 to those on this list. Responses were received from 854 business units (*i.e.*, 11 percent); among responses, 495 questionnaires were usable, yielding an overall response rate of 6.5 percent.

Analyses of respondents versus non-respondents revealed that "the industrial distribution of [the respondents] is generally similar to the industrial distribution of nonresponding COMPUSTAT business units. The responding units, however, are larger and more profitable than the nonresponding business units." (Delaney, Ichniowski, and Lewin 1988, p.11). The fact that respondents are larger than nonrespondents suggests that the respondents simply have the staff to participate in such research activities.

There are several possible reasons for the low response rate: 1) the survey was quite long—twenty-four pages—and answers to the survey questions often required specific archival data, which could discourage executives from responding, and 2) there may have been no one available in the firm to take the time needed to fill out such a lengthy questionnaire.

The response rate of 6.5 percent indicates that any inferences using these data must be made cautiously, of course. It may be the case that respondents do better at HRM activities than nonrespondents. Nonetheless, the collection of these data represent a great improvement over those that have been available to researchers to date. Most research in HRM has been limited to anecdotal evidence and case studies. Thus, the low response rate notwithstanding, this study must be seen as part of an ongoing effort, which, by virtue of these data, improves understanding of the hiring process.

## CONSTRUCTION of the VALUES INDEX

Answers to the following questions were scored on a five-point scale where one equaled NOT AT ALL and five equaled A GREAT DEAL. The variable VALUES, used in the determinants model (see Chapter Three), was set equal to the sum of the firm's answers to each of these twelve questions. Thus, each firm's score for the variable VALUES is in the range from zero to sixty.

1.  To what extent is your organization currently using EMPLOYEE INVOLVEMENT/PARTICIPATION to improve your position in the marketplace?

2.  To what extent will your organization use EMPLOYEE INVOLVEMENT/PARTICIPATION in the next several years to improve your position in the marketplace?

3.  To what extent is your organization currently using QUALITY CIRCLES to improve your position in the marketplace?

4.  To what extent will your organization use QUALITY CIRCLES in the next several years to improve your position in the marketplace?

5.  To what extent is your organization currently using EMPLOYEE TEAM-BUILDING to improve your position in the marketplace?

6.  To what extent will your organization use EMPLOYEE TEAM-BUILDING in the next several years to improve your position in the marketplace?

7.  To what extent is your organization currently using SEMI-AUTONOMOUS WORK GROUPS to improve your position in the marketplace?

8.  To what extent will your organization use SEMI-AUTONOMOUS WORK GROUPS in the next several years to improve your position in the marketplace?

9.  To what extent is your organization currently ALLOWING EMPLOYEES TO SUPERVISE THEMSELVES to improve your position in the marketplace?

10. To what extent will your organization ALLOW EMPLOYEES TO SUPERVISE THEMSELVES in the next several years to improve your position in the marketplace?

11. To what extent is your organization currently ALLOWING EMPLOYEES TO APPRAISE THEIR PEERS' PERFORMANCE to improve your position in the marketplace?

12. To what extent will your organization ALLOW EMPLOYEES TO APPRAISE THEIR PEERS' PERFORMANCE in the next several years to improve your position in the marketplace?

# CORRELATION MATRIX of VARIABLES in the DETERMINANTS MODEL

| | 1 | 2 | 3 | 4 | 5 | 6 | 7 | 8 | 9 | 10 | 11 | 12 | 13 | 14 | 15 | 16 | 17 | 18 | 19 | 20 |
|---|---|---|---|---|---|---|---|---|---|---|---|---|---|---|---|---|---|---|---|---|
| 1) HRPLAN | | | | | | | | | | | | | | | | | | | | |
| 2) RSEVAL | .24 | | | | | | | | | | | | | | | | | | | |
| 3) INTRVS | .01 | .03 | | | | | | | | | | | | | | | | | | |
| 4) SOURCES | .05 | .19 | .13 | | | | | | | | | | | | | | | | | |
| 5) TESTS | .21 | .14 | .02 | .06 | | | | | | | | | | | | | | | | |
| 6) PCTINFML | -.14 | -.08 | .02 | -.15 | .06 | | | | | | | | | | | | | | | |
| 7) SIZE | .20 | .10 | .00 | .06 | .16 | -.03 | | | | | | | | | | | | | | |
| 8) UNION | .14 | .05 | -.08 | -.31 | .36 | -.04 | .19 | | | | | | | | | | | | | |
| 9) VALUES | .26 | .08 | .08 | .07 | .17 | .04 | .14 | .10 | | | | | | | | | | | | |
| 10) TRAINING | .27 | .29 | .07 | .20 | .36 | .02 | .13 | .03 | .20 | | | | | | | | | | | |
| 11) KEXP | .06 | .04 | .18 | -.00 | .01 | .01 | -.04 | -.00 | -.01 | .06 | | | | | | | | | | |
| 12) AGMNCO | -.04 | -.09 | -.02 | -.25 | -.10 | -.04 | -.05 | -.06 | -.05 | -.14 | .06 | | | | | | | | | |
| 13) FIRE | -.02 | -.04 | .13 | .13 | -.07 | -.03 | -.04 | -.21 | -.08 | .11 | -.01 | -.01 | | | | | | | | |
| 14) TRADE | -.01 | .02 | .06 | -.01 | -.05 | .09 | .10 | -.01 | .03 | .03 | -.03 | -.07 | -.10 | | | | | | | |
| 15) TRANSP | .02 | .05 | .07 | -.12 | .42 | .05 | -.01 | .43 | .00 | .24 | .05 | -.12 | -.16 | -.12 | | | | | | |
| 16) SERVICE | .02 | .08 | .00 | .05 | -.19 | -.01 | -.03 | -.17 | -.07 | -.00 | .09 | -.09 | -.13 | -.10 | -.16 | | | | | |
| 17) MGRADE | .04 | .12 | .06 | .18 | -.05 | .02 | -.04 | -.29 | -.05 | .12 | .04 | -.06 | .35 | -.20 | .02 | .36 | | | | |
| 18) PCTMALE | -.04 | -.11 | -.08 | -.19 | .18 | -.06 | -.01 | .33 | -.05 | -.15 | -.15 | .32 | -.39 | -.18 | .20 | -.23 | -.26 | | | |
| 19) PCTWHITE | -.01 | -.08 | .00 | -.00 | .01 | -.03 | -.14 | -.10 | .03 | -.12 | -.03 | .29 | -.00 | .08 | -.02 | -.07 | .19 | .27 | | |
| 20) PCTHIGH | .00 | .09 | .09 | .22 | -.18 | -.12 | -.02 | -.35 | -.13 | .06 | .14 | .07 | .12 | -.17 | -.04 | .25 | .50 | -.17 | .08 | |
| 21) MANU | .01 | -.04 | -.06 | .11 | -.07 | -.04 | .03 | -.04 | .10 | -.19 | -.10 | -.24 | -.34 | -.26 | -.41 | -.34 | -.34 | .19 | -.12 | -.16 |

# CORRELATION MATRIX of VARIABLES in the PERFORMANCE MODEL

| | 1 | 2 | 3 | 4 | 5 | 6 | 7 | 8 | 9 | 10 | 11 | 12 | 13 | 14 | 15 | 16 |
|---|---|---|---|---|---|---|---|---|---|---|---|---|---|---|---|---|
| 1) LPROD | | | | | | | | | | | | | | | | |
| 2) HRPLAN | .01 | | | | | | | | | | | | | | | |
| 3) RSEVAL | -.02 | .24[a] | | | | | | | | | | | | | | |
| 4) TESTS | .02 | .21[a] | .14[a] | | | | | | | | | | | | | |
| 5) IPERH | .06 | .01 | .03 | .02 | | | | | | | | | | | | |
| 6) PREFINFM | .00 | -.14 | -.08 | .06 | .02 | | | | | | | | | | | |
| 7) SOURCES | .05 | .05 | .19[a] | .06 | .13[a] | -.15[a] | | | | | | | | | | |
| 8) ALABOR | -.25[a] | .34[a] | .27[a] | .30[a] | .00 | -.14[a] | .10[b] | | | | | | | | | |
| 9) TRAINING | .09[c] | .27[a] | .29[a] | .36[a] | .07 | .02 | .20[a] | .31[a] | | | | | | | | |
| 10) UNION | -.04 | .14[a] | .05 | .36[a] | -.08[c] | -.04 | -.31[a] | .40[a] | .03 | | | | | | | |
| 11) CAPITAL | .30[a] | .25[a] | .22[a] | .32[a] | .00 | -.12[b] | .13[a] | .67[a] | .42[a] | .30[a] | | | | | | |
| 12) HITECH | .01 | .02 | -.03 | -.12[b] | .01 | .02 | .13[a] | -.12[b] | -.11[b] | -.17[a] | -.11[b] | | | | | |
| 13) AGMNCO | -.04 | -.04 | -.09[c] | -.10[b] | -.02 | -.04 | -.25[a] | -.18[a] | -.14[a] | -.06 | -.10[b] | -.09[c] | | | | |
| 14) FIRE | .09[c] | -.02 | -.04 | -.07 | -.02 | -.03 | .13[a] | -.04 | .11[b] | -.21[a] | .22[a] | -.12[b] | -.10[b] | | | |
| 15) TRADE | .07 | -.01 | .02 | -.05 | .06 | .09[c] | -.01 | .07 | .03 | -.01 | -.02 | -.09[b] | -.07[c] | -.10[b] | | |
| 16) TRAN | -.01 | .02 | .05 | .42 | .07 | .05 | -.12[b] | .16[a] | .24[a] | .43[a] | .27[a] | -.15[a] | -.12[b] | -.12[a] | -.12[a] | |
| 17) SERVICE | .01 | .02 | .08[c] | -.19[a] | .00 | -.01 | .05 | -.04 | -.00 | -.17[a] | -.11[b] | -.12[a] | -.09[b] | -.10[b] | -.10[b] | -.16[a] |

[a] significant at 1 percent level
[b] significant at 5 percent level
[c] significant at 10 percent level
N-495

# References

Albrecht, James W., and B. Axell. "An Equilibrium Model of Search Unemployment." *Journal of Political Economy* 92 (1984): 824-840.

Aldrich, John H., and F.D. Nelson. *Linear Probability, Logit, and Probit Models*. Beverly Hills, CA: Sage Publications, 1984.

Arthur, Jeffrey B. "Effects of Human Resource Systems on Manufacturing Performance and Turnover." *Academy of Management Journal* 37 (1994): 670-687.

Arvey, Richard D., and R.H. Faley. *Fairness in Selecting Employees*. 2d ed. Reading, MA: Addison-Wesley, 1988.

Arvey, Richard D., and J.E. Campion. "The Employment Interview: A Summary and Review of Recent Research." *Personnel Psychology* 35 (1982): 281-322.

Asher, J., and J. Sciarrino. "Realistic Work Samples: A Review." *Personnel Psychology* 27 (1974): 519-533.

Barron, John M., John Bishop and W.C. Dunkelberg. "Employer Search." *Review of Economics and Statistics* 67 (1985): 43-52.

Barron, John M., D.A. Black, and M.A. Loewenstein. "Employer Size: The Implications for Search, Training, Capital Investment, Starting Wages, and Wage Growth." *Journal of Labor Economics* 5 (1987): 76-89.

Barron, John M., and W. Mellow. "Search Effort in the Labor Market." *Journal of Human Resources* (Summer 1979): 427-441.

Bartel, Ann P., and F.R. Lichtenberg. "The Skill Distribution and Competitive Trade Advantage of High-Technology Industries," in *Advances in Industrial and Labor Relations*, ed., D. Lewin, D. Lipsky, and D. Sockell, 161-176. Greenwich, CT: JAI Press, 1987.

Becker, Gary S. *Human Capital.* 2d ed. NY: National Bureau for Economic Research, 1975.

Bishop, John, J. Barron, and K. Hollenbeck. "Recruiting Workers: How Recruitment Policies affect the Flow of Applicants and Quality of New Workers." Columbus, OH: The National Center for Research in Vocational Education, 1983.

Breaugh, James A. "Relationships between Recruiting Sources and Employee Performance, Absenteeism, and Work Attitudes." *Academy of Management Journal* 24 (1981): 142-147.

Breaugh, J.A., and R.B. Mann. "Recruiting Source Effects: A Test of Two Alternative Explanations." *Journal of Occupational Psychology* 57 (1984): 261-267.

Brodgen, Herbert E. "When Testing Pays Off." *Personnel Psychology* 2 (1949): 171-183.

Caldwell, David F., and W. A. Spivey. "The Relationship between Recruiting Source and Employee Success: An Analysis by Race." *Personnel Psychology* 36 (1983): 67-72.

Cascio, Wayne F. "Assessing the Utility of Selection Decisions: Theoretical and Practical Considerations," in *Personnel Selection in Organizations*, ed., N. Schmitt and W. Bormann, 310-340. San Francisco, CA: Jossey-Bass, 1993.

Chandler, Alfred D., Jr. *Strategy and Structure.* Garden City, NY: Doubleday, 1962.

Clark, Kim B. "Unionization and Firm Performance: The Impact on Profits, Growth, and Productivity." *American Economic Review* 74 (1984): 893-919.

Coase, Ronald. "The Problem of Social Cost." *Journal of Law and Economics* (1960): 1-44.

Conard, M.A., and S.D. Ashworth. "Recruiting Source Effectiveness: A Meta-Analysis and Re-examination of Two Rival Hypotheses." Paper presented at the first annual meeting of the SIOP, Chicago, IL., 1986.

Craft, James. "A Critical Perspective on Human Resource Planning." *Human Resource Planning* 3, no.2 (1980): 197-211.

Datcher, Linda. "The Impact of Informal Networks on Quit Behavior." *Review of Economics and Statistics* LXV, no.3 (1983): 491-495.

Decker, Phillip, and E. Cornelius. "Note on Recruiting Sources and Job Survival Rates." *Journal of Applied Psychology* 64 (1979): 463-464.

Delaney, John Thomas, C. Ichniowski, and D. Lewin. "Environmental and Organizational Determinants of HR Planning in Organizations." Presented at the Academy of Management annual meetings, Anaheim, CA, August 1988.

———. "Employee Involvement Programs and Firm Performance," in *Proceedings of the Forty-First Annual Meeting*, ed., B.D. Dennis, 148-158. Madison, WI: Industrial Relations Research Association, 1989.

———. "Human Resource Policies and Practices in American Firms." Report submitted to the Bureau of Labor-Management Relations and Cooperative Programs, United States Department of Labor, 1989.

Devine, Theresa J., and N.M. Kiefer. "The Empirical Status of Job Search Theory." *Labor Economics* 1 (1993): 3-24.

Dipboye, Robert L. *Selection Interviews: Process Perspectives.* Cincinnati, OH: Southwestern Publishing Co., 1992.

Doeringer, Peter B., and M.J. Piore. *Internal Labor Markets and Manpower Analysis.* Lexington, MA: D.C.Heath & Company, 1971.

Draper, Norman, and H. Smith. *Applied Regression Analysis.* 2d ed. New York, NY: John Wiley and Sons, 1981.

Freeman, Richard B., and J.L. Medoff. *What Do Unions Do?.* New York, NY: Basic Books, 1984.

Gatewood, Robert D., and H. S. Feild. *Human Resource Selection.* 3d ed. New York, NY: The Dryden Press, 1994.

Gannon, M.J. "Sources of Referral and Employee Turnover." *Journal of Applied Psychology* 55 (1971): 226-228.

Ghiselli, Edwin E. "The Validity of Aptitude Tests in Personnel Selection." *Personnel Psychology* 26 (1973): 461-477.

Glueck, William F. *Personnel.* 3d ed. Plano, TX: Business Publications, Inc., 1982.

Goodmeasure, Inc. "The Changing American Workplace: Work Alternatives in the Eighties." New York, NY: American Management Association, 1985.

Hartzell, Betty. "Publisher's Letter." *Recruitment Today.* The Recruitment Supplement to *Personnel Journal.* (August 1988): 4.

Hill, R.E. "A New Look at Employee Referrals as a Recruitment Channel." *Personnel Journal* (1970): 144-148.

Holzer, Harry J. "Hiring Procedures in the Firm: Their Determinants and Outcomes," in *Human Resources and the Performance of the Firm*, ed., M.M. Kleiner, R.N. Block, M. Roomkin and S.W. Salsburg, 243-274. Madison, WI: Industrial Relations Research Association, 1987.

Hunter, John E., and F.L. Schmidt. "Ability Tests: Economic Benefits Versus the Issue of Fairness." *Industrial Relations* 21 (1982): 293-308.

———. "Quantifying the Effects of Psychological Interventions on Employee Job Performance and Workforce Productivity." *American Psychologist* 38 (1983): 473-478.

Huselid, Mark. "The Impact of Human Resource Management Practices on Turnover, Productivity, and Corporate Financial Performance." *Academy of Management Journal* (1995).

Koch, Marianne J., and G. S. Hundley. "The Effects of Unionism on Recruitment and Selection Practices," working paper (1994).

Kochan, Thomas A. *Collective Bargaining and Industrial Relations*. Homewood, IL: Richard D. Irwin, Inc., 1980.

Kohn, Meir G., and S. Shavell. "The Theory of Search." *Journal of Economic Theory* (June 1974): 665-690.

Kossek, Ellen E. "Human Resource Management Innovation." *Human Resource Management* 26 (1987): 71-92.

Landy, Frank J., Shankster, L. J. and S. S. Kohler. "Personnel Selection and Placement." *Annual Review of Psychology* 45 (1994): 261-296.

Lindquist, Victor R., and F.S. Endicott. *Northwestern Endicott Report 1986*, 40th Annual Survey. Evanston, IL: Northwestern University, 1986.

Lippman, Stephen, and J. McCall. "The Economics of Job Search: A Survey." *Economic Inquiry* 14 (1976): 155-190.

Maddala, G.S. *Econometrics*. New York, NY: McGraw-Hill Book Company, 1977.

———. *Limited Dependent and Qualitative Variables in Econometrics*. Cambridge, England: Cambridge University Press, 1983.

Malm, F. Theodore. "Recruiting Patterns of Labor Markets." *Industrial and Labor Relations Review* (1954): 507-525.

————. "Hiring Practices and Selection Standards in the San Francisco Bay Area." *Industrial and Labor Relations Review* 8 (1955): 231-252.

McCall, John J. "The Economics of Information and Job Search." *Quarterly Journal of Economics* (Feb. 1970): 113-126.

McFadden, Daniel. "Qualitative Response Variables," in *Advances in Econometrics*, ed., W. Hildebrand. Cambridge, England: Cambridge Univerity Press, 1982.

Mellow, Wesley. "Employer Size and Wages." *Review of Economics and Statistics* (August 1982): 495-501.

Miles, Robert E., and C.C. Snow. *Organizational Strategy, Structure and Process.* New York, NY: McGraw-Hill, Inc., 1978.

Milkovich, George T., and J.W. Boudreau. *Personnel/Human Resouce Management: A Diagnostic Approach.* 5th ed. Plano, TX: Business Publications Inc., 1988.

Miner, N. *Recruiting Policies and Practices.* Washington D.C.: Bureau of National Affairs, 1979.

Nkomo, Stella M. "Human Resource Planning and Organization Performance: An Exploratory Analysis." *Strategic Management Journal* 8 (1987): 387-392.

Oi, Walter Y. "Labor as a Quasi-Fixed Factor." *Journal of Political Economy* 70 (1962): 538-555.

Osterman, Paul, ed. *Internal Labor Markets.* Cambridge, MA: The MIT Press, 1984.

Peters, Thomas J., and R.H. Waterman, Jr. *In Search of Excellence.* New York, NY: Harper & Row Inc., 1983.

Quaglieri, P.L. "A Note on Variations in Recruiting Information obtained through Different Sources." *Journal of Occupational Psychology* 55 (1982): 53-55.

Rees, Albert. "Information Networks in Labor Markets." *American Economic Review* 56 (1966): 559-566.

Rees, Albert, and G.P. Schultz. *Workers and Wages in an Urban Labor Market.* Chicago, IL: University of Chicago Press, 1970.

Reid, G.L. "Job Search and the Effectiveness of Job Finding Methods." *Industrial and Labor Relations Review* 25 (1972): 479-495.

Reynolds, Lloyd. *The Structure of Labor Markets.* New York, NY: Harper and Row, 1951.

Rynes, Sara L. "Recruitment, Job Choice, and Post-Hire Consequences: A call for New Research Directions," in *Handbook of Industrial and Organizational Psychology*, ed., Dunnette, M. and L. Hough, 399-444. Palo Alto, CA: Consulting Psychologists Press, 1991.

Rynes, Sara L., and J.W. Boudreau. "College Recruiting in Large Organizations: Practice, Evaluation, and Research Implications." *Personnel Psychology* 39 (1986): 729-757.

Salop, Steven. "Systematic Job Search and Unemployment." *Review of Economic Studies* (April 1973): 191-201.

Scarpello, Vida G., and J. Ledvinka. *Personnel/Human Resource Management*. Boston, MA: PWS-Kent Publishing Co., 1988.

Schmidt, Frank L., and J.E. Hunter. "Individual Differences in Productivity: An Empirical Test of Estimates Derived from Studies of Selection Procedure Utility." *Journal of Applied Psychology* 68 (1983): 407-414.

Schmidt, Frank L., K. Pearlman, and G.S. Shane. "Further Tests of the Schmidt-Hunter Bayesian Validity Generalization Procedure." *Personnel Psychology* 32 (1979): 257-281.

Schmitt, Neal. "Social and Situational Determinants of Interview Decisions: Implications for the Employment Interview." *Personnel Psychology* 29 (1976): 79-101.

Schwab, Donald P. "Recruiting and Organizational Participation," in *Personnel Management*, ed., Rowland, K., and G. Ferris. Boston, MA: Allyn & Bacon, 1982.

Sherer, F.M. *Industrial Market Structure and Economic Performance*. 2d ed. Chicago, IL: Rand McNally College Publishing Company, 1987.

Swaroff, P.G., L.A. Barclay, and A.R. Bass. "Recruiting Sources: Another Look." *Journal of Applied Psychology* 70 (1985): 720-728.

Spence, Michael. "Job Market Signaling." *Quarterly Journal of Economics* 87 (1973): 355-374.

Taylor, H.C., and J.T. Russell. "The Relationship of Validity Coefficients to the Practical Effectiveness of Tests in Selection." *Journal of Applied Psychology* 23 (1939): 565-578.

Taylor, M.S., and D.W. Schmidt. "A Process-Oriented Investigation of Recruitment Source Effectiveness." *Personnel Psychology* 36 (1983): 343-354.

Thurow, Lester C. *Generating Inequality.* NY: Basic Books, 1975.

Turbin, Mark S., and J. G. Rosse. "Attracting and Retaining Scientists and Engineers in the High Technology Industry: A Review and Evaluation," in *Proceedings: Managing The High Technology Firm*, ed., Gomez-Mejia, L.R., and M.W. Lawless, 50-56. Boulder, CO: The Board of Regents, University of Colorado, 1988.

Ullman, J.C. "Employee Referrals: Prime Tool for Recruiting Workers." *Personnel* 43 (1966): 30-35.

U. S. Department of Labor. Bureau of Labor Statistics. *Characteristics of Major Collective Bargaining Agreements, 1977.* Bulletin, 1957.

Voos, Paula B., and L.R. Mishel. "The Union Impact on Profits: Evidence from Industry Price-Cost Margin Data." *Journal of Labor Economics* 4 (1986): 105-133.

Walker, James W. *Human Resource Planning.* New York, NY: McGraw-Hill, 1980.

————. *Human Resource Strategy.* New York, NY: McGraw-Hill, Inc., 1992.

Wanous, John P. "Organizational Entry: Newcomers Moving From Outside to Inside." *Psychological Bulletin* 84 (1977): 601-618.

————. *Organizational Entry: Recruitment, Selection, and Socialization of Newcomers.* 2d ed. Reading, MA: Addison-Wesley, 1992.

Wanous, John P., and A. Colella. "Organizational Entry Research: Current Status and Future Directions," in *Research in Personnel and Human Resource Management*, ed., K. Rowland and G. Ferris, Vol. 7. Greenwich, CT: JAI Press Inc., 1989.

Williamson, Oliver E. *Markets and Hierarchies: Analysis and Antitrust Implications*, 57-81. New York, NY: The Free Press, 1975.

# Index

For Product Safety Concerns and Information please contact our EU
representative GPSR@taylorandfrancis.com Taylor & Francis Verlag GmbH,
Kaufingerstraße 24, 80331 München, Germany

Printed and bound by CPI Group (UK) Ltd, Croydon, CR0 4YY
08/05/2025
01864468-0002